False Hope

False Hope

The Politics of Illusion in the Clinton Era

Norman Solomon

Common Courage Press · Monroe, Maine

Library of Congress Cataloging-in-Publication-Data:
Solomon, Norman, 1951—
False hope : the politics of illusion in the Clinton era / Norman
Solomon.

p.   cm.
Includes index
ISBN 1-56751-025-6 (cloth). -- ISBN 1-56751-024-8 (paper)
1. United States--Politics and government--1993- 2. Clinton,
Bill, 1946-   . I. Title.
E885.S65   1994
973.929'092--dc20   93-33893
CIP

Photo of Clinton with Kennedy, by W. Hitt, courtesy of Blackstar

I've Got to Know Words and Music by Woody Guthrie
TRO — © Copyright 1963 (Renewed) Ludlow Music, Inc., New York
Used by Permission.

Quotation from *The Trial*, Definitive Edition by Franz Kafka, trans.
by Willa and Edwin Muir. Copyright 1925, 1935, 1946 by Schocken
Books, Inc. Reprinted by permission of Schocken Books, published
by Pantheon Books, a division of Random House, Inc.

Common Courage Press
P.O. Box 702
Monroe, ME 04951
207-525-0900 fax: 207-525-3068

First Printing

Author's Note:

This book concentrates on analyzing attitudes toward the Clinton presidency among many people who were glad to see the end of the Reagan-Bush years. *False Hope* does not attempt to provide a detailed account of the various policies of the Clinton administration. Instead, the book in front of you is an essay that explores the need to move beyond false hope.

The sources for all quotes can be found in the "Notes" section (unless already specified in the text). "Notes" also includes background information and some additional comments.

I've got to know, yes, I've got to know, friend;
Hungry lips ask me wherever I go!
Comrades and friends all falling around me,
I've got to know, yes, I've got to know.

Why do your war boats ride on my waters?
Why do your death bombs fall down from my skies?
Why do you burn my farm and my town down?
I've got to know, friend, I've got to know!

What makes your boats haul death to my people?
Nitro blockbusters, big cannons and guns?
Why doesn't your ship bring food and some clothing?
I've sure got to know, folks, I've sure got to know!

Why can't my two hands get a good pay job?
I can still plow, plant, I can still sow!
Why did your lawbook chase me off my good land?
I'd sure like to know, friend, I've just got to know!

What good work did you do, sir, I'd like to ask you,
To give you my money right out of my hands?
I built your big house here to hide from my people,
Why you crave to hide so, I'd love to know!

—Woody Guthrie

"Everybody that would compromise in five minutes is the people with a real good education."

—Fannie Lou Hamer

"I have come to believe over and over again that what is most important to me must be spoken, made verbal and shared, even at the risk of having it bruised and misunderstood.... For it is not difference which immobilizes us most but silence..."

—Audre Lorde

Contents

Introduction

We have heard the trumpets. We have changed the guard. And now each in our own way, and with God's help, we must answer the call.

—the epigraph to Bill Clinton's
February 17, 1993, budget plan,
A Vision of Change for America

Some vision; some change—worse than I ever imagined. For a moment in the fall of 1992, I found myself believing that while Clinton was still a hollow, unprincipled tool of the power elite, maybe his apologists had a point. Forget that he was more-or-less endorsed by Milton Friedman (in an interview in *Forbes*, of all places), Arthur Laffer (who drew his famous curve on a napkin, creating supply-side economics), and the passionately *laissez-faire Economist* magazine. Maybe he really was some kind of social democrat, and he'd bring a touch of humaneness and reason to government. He had, after all, shed the Mondale–Dukakis austerity strategy, and spoke of investing in things and people. His numbers were laughably tiny, but they were steps in the right direction, weren't they? Even if the succession meant nothing more than a new set of snouts at the trough, maybe the torpor that characterizes official political and intellectual life might give way to a little more movement, a little more life.

All optimistic fantasies were shattered by the first fusillade of cabinet appointments, a depressing cluster of functionaries from the arms-and-austerity wing of the Democratic Party. Wall Street boardrooms were raided to staff the economic team, which would be commanded by Lloyd Bentsen, the senator from business-as-usual. Les Aspin, of all people, was trusted with the task of Cold War demobilization. Ron Brown, corporate lawyer and lobbyist for American Express and Duvalier's Haiti, would supervise a Clinton industrial policy at the Department of Commerce. Mickey Kantor, corporate lawyer, would negotiate trade deals. Warren Christopher, corporate lawyer, would oversee the New World Order. Hillary Rodham Clinton, corporate lawyer and boardmember at Wal-Mart, the low-wage retailer that's destroyed countless rural downtowns, would supervise health care.

Then the campaign's investment budget quickly became the chief executive's austerity budget. In the weeks before the inauguration, Clinton suddenly discovered the deficit problem to be much worse than he ever imagined. Official Bush administration estimates, universally viewed to be nonsense, were suddenly revealed as excessively optimistic! The summer economic plan, "Putting People First," had become a winter austerity plan—Putting Bondholders First.

Bondholders love a slow economy. It means low inflation, which preserves the value of their stock-in-trade, money. Unfortunately, most people sweat when bondholders thrive. Bondholders have loved the Clinton administration. In the ten months following the election, bond prices rose 20 percent. Employment is barely up, and real income is down, but the folks at Goldman Sachs, the bond house that paid Clinton's economic czar Robert Rubin $17 million in 1992 to be its co-chair, are very happy.

Introduction

During the campaign, Clinton said the economy was suffering not a mere recession, but a long-term illness, among whose symptoms is the 16 percent decline in real hourly wages over the last twenty years—a period when real Gross Domestic Product has grown by more than half.

But "real" wages—the average wage adjusted for inflation—are a statistical abstraction. More pungent measures are available. Since 1973, the time necessary for a worker paid the average hourly wage to earn the average household's yearly expenses has grown 43 percent; to buy the average new house, 45 percent; to buy the average new car, 57 percent; and to pay for a year at Yale or the University of California, 75 percent.[1] People don't throw about such numbers in public because it would be an unflattering judgment on this supposed prosperity machine. This is a pretty sorry performance for the system that is supposed to have been the one that proved Marx wrong, the one that promised endless upward mobility for the masses instead of harder work and greater insecurity for less pay.

The state stripped bare

Since the start of 1993, all public talk of economic policy was narrowed into deficit reduction. There were only two choices: the Clinton plan, or some vague and no doubt cruel Republican scheme. Campaign promises of investment and renewal were scrapped. Peanuts were offered for military-to-civilian conversion, described by Ron Brown as the "cornerstone" of the regime's economic policy, and the Environmental Protection Agency will take an 8 percent real budget cut. Revenue from stiffer taxes on the wealthy, a truly fine thing, will go into deficit reduction, not energy research or public housing. Fairness, alas, dictates pointing to the expansion of the Earned Income Tax Credit, a significant benefit for the working poor (that cynically could be seen as a well-disguised subsidy to low-wage employers).

But the overall effect of the budget, by restricting spending and increasing taxes, will be to slow the economy for years to come. Other spending cuts promised for late 1993 and beyond, will slow things further. Never in U.S. history have we been subject to a decade of steady fiscal stringency like this: the budget turned tight in the late 1980s, and is likely to stay that way through the late 1990s, barring a revolution.

This shouldn't have been a surprise. Clinton's own budgets in Arkansas gave no evidence of fiscal imagination; he ran a very tight ship, and showed a great fondness for user fees, like tuition at state universities. These are fairly regressive substitutes for tax increases. The state tax system, Citizens for Tax Justice figures show, is stingingly regressive— the poorest fifth of the population is taxed at a rate two-thirds higher than the richest 1 percent.

I dwell on fiscal matters because it's my beat, but also because, in the words of a German sociologist, Rudolf Goldscheid, "the budget is the skeleton of the state stripped of all misleading ideologies."[2]

Clinton still sounds all his rhetoric about fundamental change, innovation, reinvention. But he also told us to watch the bond market. The bond market sees economic stagnation and political stability for years to come.

Clinton, it is universally agreed, was elected to fix

the economy. In mainstream speech, the "economy" is always approached as a realm in itself, a domain for experts, set off from the rest of social life. In the papers, most economic news is relegated to the business pages, a placement that reveals whose interests are being served by the reporting, and which helps seal a good bit of truth off from a broader public. But here, from two perspectives, top and bottom, are the fundamental problems of the U.S. economy.

From the top...

From a mainstream, top-down point of view, growth is too slow, and domestic profits too weak, to justify high levels of productive investment. The share of GDP devoted to investment in plant and equipment, which has been shown to be tightly associated with overall economic growth rates, is one of the lowest in the First World. The managers of the national capital build office buildings—or used to, in the 1980s, until most urban real estate markets crashed—but are barely replacing real productive assets as they deteriorate. Here, that is. They invest abroad at enthusiastic rates, not merely in low-wage countries like Mexico, but in high-wage ones like Europe.

It's not only private investment that is weak by First World standards. During the 1980s, government in the U.S. invested only 0.3 percent of GDP in civilian physical infrastructure, compared with 3.7 percent in Germany and 5.7 percent in Japan. Reaching German levels of public investment would require a boost of $200 billion, and Japan, $324 billion, in U.S. spending.

Changing this would require severe strictures on Wall Street, imaginative rethinking of the role of pension funds (which are huge pools of workers' savings that are held and managed by big capital), large taxes on financial assets held by rich people and institutional investors, a huge boost in public investment spending, the creation of new public and cooperative financial institutions, controls on international trade and capital flows, experiments with different forms of corporate ownership and governance. Of course, a regime populated by Ron Brown and Bob Rubin will do none of these things.

What we've gotten so far is a tight budget with investment cuts, in the interest of Wall Street, and plans for big federal layoffs in the name of "reinventing government"—an ideal environment for financial assets, but little else. After increasing under Bush(!), the U.S. public investment budget will decline in 1994, according to a study by Todd Schaefer of the Economic Policy Institute.[3] As for control over capital and trade flows, Clinton has enthusiastically adopted Bush's North American Free Trade Agreement and the rest of the bipartisan free-trade agenda, which holds that the entire globe should be a free-fire zone for multinational capital.

Over the years, Clintonites have talked about something like an "industrial policy"—coordinated, public–private schemes to support industrial and technological development—though the phrase is avoided now as unfashionably anti-market and *dirigiste.* Though more designed to increase corporate profitability than raise living standards, it is a more rational way to run capitalism, and could mark a minor increase in the level of social control over investment.

We haven't yet seen much in this area from first-year Clintonites. But we can time travel back to Arkansas for clues. An excellent June 29, 1992, piece in the *Los Angeles Times* by Michael J. Goodman and John M. Broder says almost all you need to know. "Presidential candidate Bill Clinton has rewarded the financial elite of Arkansas with lucrative state business and low-interest loans while soliciting them—in one instance urgently and personally—for millions of dollars in political contributions and campaign loans," the story began. It went on to document intimate relations among a "pool of loan recipients and bankers, bond brokers and attorneys" around the Arkansas Development Finance Authority. (Bond brokers and attorneys—just like the Clinton cabinet of 1993!) While enriching themselves, they claim to have created 2,700 jobs over seven years, or one a day. An executive of Stephens Inc., the Little Rock investment firm with deep ties to both Bill and Hillary, said that the governor had set up the authority so as to assure "total control," thereby "politiciz[ing] the bond selling process."

Clinton's treasury extended $400 million in corporate tax breaks, a fifth of the impoverished state's budget. He showed a special fondness for the state's chicken industry, an industry that keeps its farmers in near-indentured servitude, that works its underpaid, frequently injured workers at an extraordinary pace, that discharges half a million tons of chicken-shit into Arkansas' rivers every year, and which marinates its products in salmonella-tinged concoctions before shipping them.[4] It's always energizing to recall the Arkansas anecdotes; they're a fine pre-emptive antidote to the strain of Clinton apologias that mourn the way his inner liberal has been frustrated by bad external forces. Moving from broiler barons to bond barons is undeniably a step up the social ladder, but the principles are the same.

...and the bottom

From the bottom, this country produces appalling levels of poverty and social polarization. There's an international collaborative effort called the Luxembourg Income Study (LIS) that, for the last decade, has been gathering statistics on income distribution and poverty around the First World, and analyzing them, too. It shows that by almost every measure, the U.S. has the highest poverty level and most unequal distribution of income in the Northern Hemisphere.

A word about the politics of defining poverty. The U.S. poverty line was set in the early 1960s, based on early 1950s research. That research showed that the average household spent one-third of its income on food, therefore, the poverty line should be set at three times the minimum food budget. That line has simply been adjusted for inflation ever since. This reflects the center-right notion that poverty is an absolute level of minimum consumption that doesn't change over time. (As the Thatcherites put it, today's poor person is far better off than the average Victorian was.) No allowance is made for the rise in average incomes, or changes in the market basket or social norms over time. Patricia Ruggles of the Urban Institute re-figured the poverty line based on modern spending patterns—health care and child care, for example—and found that 24 percent of the U.S. population would be poor by a modern definition, twice the official levels.

Like many other studies of poverty, the LIS uses another standard to define the poverty line: people with incomes (after taxes and welfare payments) less than half the average are poor. By that standard, in the mid-1980s, 19.8 percent of Americans were poor, compared with 12.4 percent in Canada, 6.6 percent in Germany, and 5.8 percent in Sweden. Our poor are also very poor; it would take a 36.7 percent increase in their income to bring them all up to the poverty line, the highest of the eight countries studied.[5]

Not only do we excel in overall poverty, we excel in the subspecialties as well. In all countries, single-mother families are the poorest household type. Women earn lousy wages, have a hard time getting full-time employment, and are expected to take care of the kids, too. In the U.S., during the early 1980s (sorry, but this is the most recent data available), single-mother families had incomes 54 percent of two-earner families, compared with 59 percent in Canada, 76 percent in France, and 84 percent in Sweden. Surprisingly, however, a large portion of U.S. single mothers are in the labor force (at work or looking for it)—71 percent, the third-highest of eight countries studied, after Sweden and Norway. Reasons for the higher incomes and employment rates among Scandinavian women include public child care, seriously pursued legal assurances of gender equality, and high unionization rates. German single mothers have higher relative incomes, even though fewer than 60 percent of them are in the labor force.[6]

Wage "dispersion"—a cute euphemism that economists prefer to inequality, since it suspends value judgments—in the U.S. is also a remarkable thing. The U.S. started the 1980s with the most unequal distribution of wages among seventeen nations studied by the Organization for Economic Cooperation and Development (OECD, a Paris-based official think tank sponsored by twenty-four rich industrial countries). From these already high levels, the U.S. experienced the second-highest increase in wage inequality, after Britain, among the seventeen.

Why did it happen? The OECD trots out a few explanations, some of which you may have heard on the news, and none of which holds much explanatory power. It can't be that an influx of young people into the labor force (one favored explanation) depressed wages, since the OECD's index of the number of young people in the labor force shows their ranks thinner in eight countries, unchanged in two, and up in only three, and there by an average of only 5 percent. It can't be deindustrialization, either; inequality increased within industries in most countries. An alleged shortage of skilled labor, which might drive up high-end wages as employers bid up wages in the face of short supplies; the number of college-educated workers increased in most countries. Demographic explanations don't fly either; inequality within demographic groups—people of the same age and occupation, or same educational level, or family status, or work experience— increased in several countries studied. The OECD explains this by "an increased importance of skills not well measured by educational qualifications, such as the ability to work with other people." Mystery solved! The reason for polarization: "does not work well with others."

The countries that didn't experience an increase in wage inequality during the 1980s—Denmark, Finland, Germany, Italy, and Norway — are ones with strong centralized wage-setting mechanisms, like national multi-industry bargaining. Formal and informal pay-setting schemes were scrapped or weakened in several countries that saw an increase in wage inequality—Australia, Britain, Spain, and Sweden. Minimum wages eroded in others that showed more "dispersion"—Canada, France, Portugal, Spain, and the United States. Another culprit, the OECD barely concedes, is the decline in unionization. Wage setting, then, was exposed more nakedly to market forces, and "dispersion" was the natural result.[7]

So what would it take to reverse these polarizing, immiserating trends? To start with, a civilized minimum income, vigorous comparable worth and affirmative action programs, a publicly funded child care system, higher levels of unionization, and a more collective wage-setting strategy. All of this is quite expensive. An administration led by a deficit-cutter who defended his state's union-destroying right-to-work law, and then bragged about it in economic development ads while he was governor, is not likely to lead the charge in any of these areas. Clinton promises to end welfare as we know it, but the money necessary to do this right—to fund child care and job creation schemes—won't be forthcoming.

FALSE HOPE

Believe it or not, one of Clinton's lead thinkers on poverty is none other than Bob Rubin, the $17 million man from Goldman Sachs, where he is sure to have learned much about poverty. But it's not just conservative Democrats who think Rubin knows his poverty; even great urban liberals do. Mario Cuomo had Rubin lead the team that wrote the "challenge of inner city poverty" chapter for the second report of the Cuomo Commission on Competitiveness. Here, incredibly, is Rubin et al.'s "integrated strategy" for economic inclusion. "The public and private sectors [should] provide [a] helping hand by implementing a *community-based self-help strategy*." No money in that outstretched hand; just an offer of self-help. And what are the ingredients of this strategy? Prenatal care, immunization programs, preschool programs, "developmentally appropriate school reforms" (including sensitivity training), school-based clinics, mentoring programs in the middle schools, "youth centers for struggling high-school students and dropouts as well as second-chance centers for adults who require additional help to gain their diplomas," expanded apprenticeship programs, private sector advisory committees, demonstration programs, mentoring programs in business, stepping up the war on drugs, and, last, a public employment program.[8] The Clinton administration has ruled out the public jobs program (it was probably put in there to satisfy a noisy unionist on the poverty team); the rest of the program's ingredients are either superficial, symbolic, or punitive. No sign of serious money, of course.

Semi-cheerful coda

And I've only begun to scratch the surface—nothing about the maintenance of the U.S. imperium fundamentally intact, despite some base closings and arms cutbacks; the willingness to kill Somalis for no apparent reason (except maybe to restore the exploration rights of several U.S. oil companies interrupted by chaos and war); an indifference to civil rights, and a willingness to play to the bigotry of Rush Limbaugh's America on welfare and crime; the endless compromises and betrayals (Haitians, lesbians and gays, Lani Guinier). It's been said of Clinton that if you put him in a room with twenty people, eighteen of whom agree with him, he'll try to cut deals with the other two. All the noise so far is coming from the right, and that's who he'll compromise with.

The left, such as it is, has partly silenced itself in the name of giving Clinton a chance. I'll leave it to Norman Solomon to describe the rich mechanisms of self-deception and self-censorship that lead to this—the eagerness to give Bill a chance, to keep quiet in the hope of remaining a player, all the other silly excuses. The broader delusion is that Clinton is just a bad Democrat, one of the principal forces in its drive to the right, but that the party itself is redeemable. To believe this you'd have to forget the intimate ties between corporate America and the congressional Democrats, or the miserable urban Democrats who run our big cities, hacks utterly in the grip of local real estate and banking interests who promote downtown development above all else.

But sometimes self-delusions are junked, self-censorship is broken, and marvelous things can happen. Maybe the bond market is wrong; markets are usually wrong when they are at extremes, and the bond market has gone to extremes. Maybe it isn't all stagnation and stasis. When it began looking like Clinton would win, I dusted off my copy of Garry Wills's *Nixon Agonistes.* Wills recalled that in the early 1960s, people had hoped that the replacement of the tired old Eisenhower crowd with a crew of Harvard whiz-bangs would transform everything. "Under Eisenhower," Wills wrote, "one could still claim that a person (Dulles, say) or an aberrant policy (massive retaliation) was at fault. These were lapses in a System, a System which could be tinkered with. But under Kennedy, if things were wrong, it was not because the wrong party or the wrong man was in charge of the System; the fault must be in the System itself."[9]

People are a little less naïve about the System now, more willing to believe the worst of it. Clinton is nothing if not a tinkerer. But there's no reason to believe that the new gang of Yale whiz-bangs can do better than the Harvard models of the early 1960s. Must be the System then.

—Doug Henwood
September 11, 1993

Notes

1. All figures computed by the writer from data provided by the U.S. Bureau of Labor Statistics, the Motor Vehicle Manufacturers Association, the National Association of Realtors, Yale University, and UCLA.

2. Quoted in Joseph Schumpeter, "The Crisis of the Tax State," *International Economic Papers* 4 (1954), p. 7.

3. Todd Schaefer, "Still Neglecting Public Investment: The FY94 Budget Outlook," Economic Policy Institute Briefing Paper (Washington, D.C.: Economic Policy Institute, September 1993).

4. Michael J. Goodman and John M. Broder, "Clinton's Rein on Bonds Linked to Contributions: Finance authority he controls formed a pool of moneyed elite that's often tapped for campaign funds," *Los Angeles Times*, June 29, 1992, p. A1; Doug Henwood, "The change agents," *Left Business Observer* #54, August 4, 1992, p. 1.

5. Lea Achdut and Orit Kristal, "Poverty in an International Perspective: A Re-examination," Luxembourg Income Study Working Paper #95, March 1993.

6. Yin-Ling Irene Wong, Irwin Garfinkel, and Sara McLanahan, "Single Mother Families in Eight Countries: Economic Status and Social Policy," Luxembourg Income Study Working Paper #76, April 1992.

7. Organization for Economic Cooperation and Development, *Employment Outlook* (Paris: OECD, July 1993).

8. Cuomo Commission on Competitiveness, *America's Agenda: Rebuilding Economic Strength* (Armonk, N.Y.: M.E. Sharpe, 1992), pp. 124-56.

9. Quoted in Henwood, *Left Business Observer* #54, p. 3.

One

And the Invisible Hand Plays On

The most common stories of American politics are akin to fairy tales—endlessly repeated by mass media, and accepted in the internal worlds of individuals. The story tellers may be blamed; yet it is the credulity of the story believers that makes the charade possible. Complete with dramatic noises and plenty of posturing, the highly publicized conflicts along Pennsylvania Avenue have much in common with bogus wrestling matches on TV.

"The Republicans," observed *New York Times* eminence Thomas L. Friedman exactly five months after Bill Clinton's inauguration, are "in an awkward situation. Surely, many of them must think Mr. Clinton is going in the right direction—the only direction available—even if they don't approve of every turn. But they can't afford politically to give him credit for it." Wrangling over budgets, Washington mostly fine-tunes. The fat cats of U.S. politics swallowed a big canary in President Clinton, and are not so indiscreet as to burp, or gloat, too loudly. Why risk goading somnolent liberals on Capitol Hill and elsewhere? No need to disrupt their cautious reveries.

The image of Clinton battling the status quo

can foster a sense of pride in the president for people who found the previous dozen years to be dispiriting. The chance to feel good—or at least better—about the USA's top leadership has wide appeal. Twelve rapacious years can be seen as a long nightmare from which we are now awakening, an ordeal we survived. Important differences exist between the Clinton team and its Republican predecessors on some issues. And, after a long line of wooden chief executives, Bill Clinton seems less programmed, more like a real person.

But often, focusing on the president's personality and intimate proclivities, the news media escort us into a swamp of clichés. Wallowing in them keeps us off the political streets and out of trouble, where incisive analysis and action might find progressive voice. We're encouraged to consider the president in personalized terms, so that the political horizons of the country seem to be overshadowed by a never-ending procession of historic personas. Yet, as Mark Crispin Miller has put it, "this image of the mighty individual is a corporate fiction, the careful work of committees and think tanks, repeatedly reprocessed by the television industry for daily distribution to a mass audience." The well-known faces are painted on the shells of a game in which the invisible hand is always quicker than the eye.

In the United States, the political midway is lined with shell games. For twelve Reagan-Bush years a mythos grew that two basic camps were arrayed against each other. One side was united by its dislike for Reagan and Bush policies; but within that camp were very different analyses. Was the main problem that deplorable people had gained power, or that their ascendancy had made a destructive system even worse? Such questions may have seemed unimportant or academic while conservative Republicans ran the White House. Now that a Democrat has taken up residence, however, the analysis becomes crucial. It determines, in effect, whether well-meaning people will deceive themselves in the mid-1990s about the nature of the government and its presidential leadership.

II

If Bill Clinton did not exist, it would have been necessary to invent someone like him. In a manner of speaking, he *was* invented: by his longtime backers at the Democratic Leadership Council, co-founded by Clinton in the mid-1980s and funded by such "middle class" bastions as the top echelons of Arco, Prudential-Bache, Dow Chemical, Georgia Pacific, the American Petroleum Institute and Martin Marietta. They boosted Clinton in tandem with the news media that pronounced him the front-runner for the Democratic presidential nomination before a single vote was cast in the 1992 primaries.

As a devotee of hyper-pragmatism, Clinton connected with key demographic and economic trends. "Fiscal conservatism and social liberalism proved to be an effective campaign formula," the *Washington Post*'s Hobart Rowen noted after the 1992 general election ("fiscal conservatism" being a lovely euphemism for harmony with extreme inequities and unequal opportunities). Candidate Clinton spoke to the perceived needs of large numbers of baby boomers and their kids—eager for important personal freedoms in areas such as abortion and lesbian/gay rights, and worried about specters of financial insecurity in the United States. President Clinton has gambled that many supporters grateful for his "social liberalism" won't challenge other parts of his political formula: such as economic stratification remaining firmly in place, and foreign policies closely resembling those of Republican presidents he used to denounce.

Behind the celebrated facades of American "democracy," elites go about their business of grooming hired help for high elective offices. Movers-and-shakers of the Democratic Party put their heads together—gathering at the Virginia estate of Pamela Harriman in the lead-up to the 1992 campaign—developing plans and raising millions to propel a new wave of national party leaders. Days after the '92 electoral victory, the former domestic policy director at the Carter White House, Stuart Eizenstat, was adulatory about the coalescence hosted by Harriman: "I can't emphasize how important that was in moving the party to center: a tougher defense policy, the focus on the middle class, the self-examination of where and why we'd gone wrong. It led to the kind of direction Clinton took the party."

Fast forward seven months: In the White House Rose Garden, standing next to his new appointee as top media strategist and adviser, Clinton said that the selection of David Gergen "signals to the American people where I am, what I believe and what I'm going to do." Although a dozen years of right-wing excesses had a wide array of Democrats talking the talk of fairness and denouncing undue deference to the rich, their loyal opposition to

And the Invisible Hand Plays On

Reaganomics was more loyalty than opposition—a fact symbolized by the prominence in the Clinton administration of Treasury Secretary Lloyd Bentsen and former Reagan PR flack Gergen, two of the men in Washington most responsible for promoting huge federal giveaways to the wealthy during the 1980s.

Epitomizing the narrow non-debate that can seem quite contentious, Gergen and liberal columnist Mark Shields squared off for six years on the "MacNeil/Lehrer NewsHour," as if they represented the alpha and omega of the nation's political universe. When Gergen returned to the White House at the end of spring 1993, near-unanimous mass media praise greeted the appointment, lauded as reflecting the new president's return to centrist sanity. *Newsweek* hailed Clinton's "shift to the right" and prodded him to show "the backbone" to stay there. An errant *New York Times* editorial, critical of Gergen's record, drew an angry response from Gergen's sparring partner: Shields wrote in his *Washington Post* column—headlined "The David Gergen I Know"—that the *Times* had published "a truly hysterical editorial" amounting to "political debate descended to character assassination." Shields declared that the former Reagan operative "knows something about successful presidential leadership.... What Gergen offers and what Clinton needs is a reality check: the able, honest, smart guy who will speak truth to power." Mahatma Gergen to the rescue.

Earlier in the spring Gergen had publicly faulted the new administration for "emphasizing tax increases over spending cuts"—a predictable admonition from someone who'd worked at President

Reagan's side. Before agreeing to go to work for President Clinton, according to *Newsweek*, Gergen "reportedly secured a promise from Clinton that he would adhere to a moderate political course." But whatever agreement the two may have reached, Bill Clinton's presidency settled into a groove that David Gergen could find suitably "moderate."

As he got acclimated to the Oval Office, Clinton showed himself willing time and again to kiss the rings of "deficit-cutters," while budgets shredded dreams of a new direction for the country. With little debate in mass media (and with notable assists from the likes of Ross Perot, Paul Tsongas and Warren Rudman, along with the Clinton-Gore duo), the theology of slashing government budgets to decrease social spending is no longer just the Republican credo. It is now the true faith, opposed only by political heretics. "The deficit" is the devil; a stake must be driven through its bleeding heart by cutting government expenditures such as dreaded "entitlements." Business, aided by government, is to be our salvation. The propagation of such beliefs is necessary to sanctify the federal priorities that benefit the rich—who are anxious to see the government tighten its belt and loosen their own.

Much has been made of Bill Clinton as the symbol of a new generation—at one time riddled with dissent and even rebellion—now coming to power in the United States. But how you view Clinton depends largely on how you would prefer to interpret the parable of his life, intertwined as it is with the baby-boom generation and its winding road to the 1990s.

Two

'60s Memories, '90s Distress

When Bill Clinton put his hand on the inaugural Bible, he embodied fresh leadership—promising to help the nation shake off an era of stagnation, dishonesty and greed. None of the supporters of the new president figured more prominently in his political calculus than men and women of his own generation. To a lot of them—and to many of their parents and children—Clinton represented the possibility of turning frustrated hopes into realities.

During the last decade of the century, it was logical that political products would be extensively tailored to fit people in their middle years. Aiming at the huge first generation born after World War Two, Bill Clinton connected with common preoccupations. For many baby boomers, high hopes have collided with repeated disappointments; perhaps that's an unavoidable collision for most people of any generation, but boomers grew up feeling somehow special—and have been, if only by dint of numbers: 76 million Americans born between 1946 and 1964. From advertising to politicking, such demographics draw inordinate attention. As a politician, Clinton seemed to be selling what most baby boomers could welcome in a president: pleasant rhetoric that indicates humanistic priorities across the board, combined with policies that appear to advance their personal interests.

Bill Clinton offered his generation a political path paved with modern technology and few restrictions on personal life. He spoke of an enticing future—rapid advancement for new-era professionals and other Americans aspiring to such status. Amid a profusion of cutting-edge computers, information superhighways and the like, a high-tech horizon would lead us away from a bleak economic landscape. What's more, we wouldn't have to succumb to uptight authority figures, as Clinton himself made clear; energetic and able to look spontaneous, he was obviously more at ease with sexuality and less rigid with his own body armor than his Republican foes. Clinton could evoke a future of tolerant prosperity into the 21st century.

Clinton ran on a 1992 platform titled "A New Covenant with the American People"—a sort of revised social contract. The fine print would be hard to read, overshadowed as it was by so much rhetorical camouflage. Painful legacies of history were reduced to a series of unfortunate accidents; in a typical passage, the '92 Democratic Party platform pledged to "restore the covenant that welfare was meant to be: a promise of temporary help for people who have fallen on hard times"—*fallen,* as if families languishing in poverty had not been pushed and shoved, for a very long time. The call for "*temporary* help" echoed the attitude that social spending should be curtailed.

Beneath the glossy chimera of high-tech

progress, many people simply would be excluded from the goodies. Clinton's frequent refrains about opportunity for all, accompanied by a few tepid reform scenarios, hardly threatened to disrupt the vast economic disparities in place across the United States. When hiring occurs for the ballyhooed high-pay jobs, it doesn't take a social scientist to know that poor people will be at the end of the line; they'll be free to work at McDonald's or Burger King. (Of course exceptions are liable to be much remarked upon; the ghetto resident who founds a software firm must be publicized, much like a gas station attendant who wins at Super Lotto.) For tens of millions of people in the United States, an unwritten "No Admittance" sign hangs over the promised land of prosperity.

During the 1992 Democratic National Convention, I found myself in a TV-studio green room with Norman Ornstein, the American Enterprise Institute savant who often appears on the tube as an expert on political matters. "Well, looks like you've finally got the Democratic Party you've been wanting all these years," I said. He nodded, and I went on: "And what about poor people? Where are they supposed to go now?" Ornstein barely glanced up from his finger food. "Poor people don't do very much anyway," he replied.

For most baby boomers in the mid-1990s, concerns about poor people are unlikely to be much higher on their agenda than on Norman Ornstein's, or Bill Clinton's. In media parlance and in political calculation, the most important baby boomers have some money and want more, or used to have some money and want it back. In the battles between elite factions (sometimes referred to as influential Democrats and Republicans), poor people are—more than ever—virtually ignored in national politics. For many political analysts who may have expressed more concern about them in the past, the poor are now passé. Voicing conventional wisdom among Washington pundits, liberal columnist Christopher Matthews—a former aide to House Speaker Tip O'Neill—said on network television in April 1993: "The country is not clamoring for a jobs bill." Complacently self-reinforcing, such pronouncements depict the unemployed and minimally employed poor as irrelevant in the corridors of power.

Harping on "the middle class," Clinton has concentrated on speaking to the diminished expectations of people who grew up in a rosier postwar era. On the way to 1600 Pennsylvania Avenue, and after moving in, Clinton has been careful to give more emphasis to the poor's "responsibility" to the government than vice versa. And, to the benefit of his "New Democrat" credentials, he has avoided making common cause with blacks and Latinos and Native Americans and others still burdened by the awful weight of history in the present day. With much of Clinton's message conveyed by omission, poverty is not to be ranked as a crisis.

Often we've been told that Bill Clinton is an archetype for his generation, arriving at the pinnacles of power in the 1990s. Meanwhile, concentric challenges have been emerging: to reassess how we make priorities in our personal lives as well as how we relate to politics. With so many years of Republican presidencies finally behind us, the political terrain ahead might seem markedly changed. Yet our view of the near future is inevitably tinted by our window on the past.

II

Bill Clinton's election as president symbolized a generational changing of the guard, but it also represented a way to square the spiral that many people in his generation had traveled: from '60s memories to '90s distress. Each of our lives, moving through personal and historic crossroads, keeps encountering options that can be difficult or impossible to reconcile: risk and caution, growth and security, the enlivening and the usual, authenticity and imitation, deeper expression or easier passivity; evocation of what might be, or accommodation to powers-that-be.

The heights of euphoria during the '60s are frequently matched by the depths of a sense of loss now. Those of us who felt we were coming of age a quarter-century ago might not speak aloud about such feelings of loss, or even think about them, these days. (Many of us are too busy.) Maybe we've been no less adept at burying troublesome emotions than our elders were, to our often-righteous distaste, long ago. Many of the best hopes that flowered during the late 1960s have gone to seed, bouncing along the hard ground of "realism" and rigidity. But maybe we're now still mourning, as if wondering why the earth stopped opening.

The Reagan and Bush presidencies, at odds with so much and so many, gave way to a new leader committed to occupying middle grounds. Personable and comfortable with youthful mass-culture symbols, Bill Clinton resonates with many of his generation; he is in sync with common evasions. A popular spin asserts that he has embraced pragmatism without abandoning principles. He has squared the spiral, discarding his past dissent without renouncing it—for instance, endorsing military assaults that took uncounted Iraqi lives in early 1991, and giving orders to take a few more for good measure in mid-1993—without repenting prior opposition to the Vietnam War.

As his administration continued, Clinton and many supportive baby boomers helped to justify each other, amid mounting evidence that he could talk ideals and jettison them with equal aplomb. A half-year into his presidency, the list of Clinton's obvious betrayals was long enough to disturb anyone left of dead-center; yet there was widespread reticence to move beyond equivocal expressions of concern. Sure, the patterns of presidential compromises were disheartening. "But if Clinton becomes the nation's scapegoat, progressives are likely to be added to the fire as sacrificial lambs," *Mother Jones* magazine fretted in summer 1993, in an editor's note by Jeffrey Klein. "My generation is particularly at risk, since he could be our best and brightest offering."

Finding excuses for Clinton's compromises, we excuse our own; and vice versa. Giving ourselves the benefit of doubts that would be better explored than shut down or glossed over, we do the same for him. For a fleeting moment he was once among the best of us, publicly opposing an immoral war; now he is closer to the worst, going along to get along with a massive death industry's five-sided edifice and mega-finance matrix. At one time, the cries of the poor, near and far, were heard and amplified, their anguish deemed meaningful, even intolerable; now, in the middle ages of the 1990s, so often, ambitious ears are tuned only to hear a different pitch. Sensitivity may be worn on the sleeve, but realpolitik expediencies keep occupying the mind.

By now, media are accustomed to discussing how "the '60s" affected Bill Clinton and others of his generation who have taken power in recent years. Whether or not we can personally remember the 1960s, they are "remembered" for us by a profusion of marketed memories hyping and mythologizing that bygone time, as if into submission—muting an era that, at its best, rejected mass-produced substitutions for one's own experience. Intense human connections went hand in hand with attempts to interrupt "normal" dissembling. But today, reminders of those earlier times may seem like jagged bits of black vinyl, a shattered long-playing record that one might see along the side of a road, shards of past vitality neither absent nor present, even the label faded beyond significance.

III

Numbness keeps people from questioning too much. Yet the status quo need not numb or block feeling as much as guide it; the ambient noises of media and politics are apt to confine sympathies to circumscribed realms. Emotion and empathy per se are not discouraged—*inappropriately focused* emotion and empathy are. (Empathize with dying Kurdish babies in Iraq, but not with dying Kurdish babies in Turkey—and not with Iraqi children dying because of U.S. government actions. How soon do you suppose that a Hollywood film or made-for-TV network movie in the USA will focus on the suffering of Iraqis under U.S. bombardment?) With a mass-media process homogenizing so much in the United States, the absence of a clear sense of oneself accentuates vulnerability to traditional pressures, and pervasive myths.

Yet myths and public pretenses go only so far. Sooner or later, past and present might converge in the loneliest of nights, roiled with disappointments of wanting to live one way but finding ourselves ensnared in another. Unpleasant legacies can cling, and even suffocate. Inevitably, the poisons and possibilities in the air affect people of any generation. The destructive powers of the dominant culture can be as stealthy as cat burglars, stealing our best dreams while we sleep.

In the midst of all this, politicians offer us the promise of better days.

Three

JFK, Clinton
and the
Politics of Myth

Six months before Bill Clinton became president, I stood in the press gallery of Madison Square Garden, above the colorful pastiche of the Democratic National Convention, as thousands of delegates—and millions of TV viewers across the country—watched a carefully crafted movie about Bill Clinton's life. Suddenly, on screen, a teenage Bill appeared in the Rose Garden of the White House, shaking hands with President Kennedy. The blurry footage lasted only a few seconds, yet its effect was electrifying: A thunderclap struck; in an instant the delegates went wild, their delirium shaking the huge convention hall. Like some pre-planned spontaneous combustion, both orchestrated and authentic, the explosive response seemed to be insisting on making history. Political manifest destiny was in the air. A torch was being passed, over our heads.

To a great extent, John F. Kennedy's heroic image comes from how he spoke. Kennedy can be remembered most fondly for words and appearance; at a time when the TV age was young, he came across as articulate and comfortable, even urbane, on screen (unlike the sweaty and dour Richard Nixon, a crucial difference for the 1960 election). The enduring lines are majestic, almost Shakespearean; in retrospect, for the emotive substance of America's political memory, JFK achieved most in the first few minutes of his presidency:

"Let the word go forth from this time and place, to friend and foe alike, that the torch has been passed to a new generation of Americans—born in this century, tempered by war, disciplined by a hard and bitter peace, proud of our ancient heritage—and unwilling to witness or permit the slow undoing of those human rights to which this Nation has always been committed, and to which we are committed today at home and around the world."

"All this will not be finished in the first one hundred days. Nor will it be finished in the first one thousand days, nor in the life of this Administration, nor even perhaps in our lifetime on this planet. But let us begin."

"And so, my fellow Americans, ask not what your country can do for you—ask what you can do for your country."

A purpose of such rapturous oratory was to induce a kind of prolonged swoon—speech as seduction, carried to new heights. Firm resonant voice delivering patriotically-charged poetic lines, forefinger jamming the air, youthful man rugged and erudite—he was a new president out of central casting, and as it happened the first president born in the 20th century. In public realms, with politics largely about the riches of symbology, JFK was loaded.

JFK, Clinton and the Politics of Myth

The shocking assassination transformed John Kennedy into instant mega-nostalgia, and more: He rapidly became a deity, above and beyond the customary patrimony of presidents, with ascent to the political heavens as swift as a NASA booster rocket. From then on, JFK was to be the prototype for a myriad of political rescue fantasies; to many American minds, a raft of subsequent national dysfunctions and disasters could be dated from his untimely departure from our midst. (One effect was to encourage citizens to focus on politician-heroes as superstar personalities, so that viewing the USA's history-as-it-happens could entail becoming more passively childlike than ever. It was almost as if the head of a beloved TV household, the Andersons or the Cleavers, had been taken from us suddenly, senselessly, at the height of their relevance; Jimmy and Ward, we hardly knew ye.) In the secure tragisweetness of memory, we could always mourn the loss of JFK, and imagine how he might have set things right had he lived—a yearning understandable in children, yet prone to grow attenuated and even pathetic among adults.

Twenty-five years after John Kennedy's death, former president Jimmy Carter used his speech at the 1988 Democratic Convention to egg on the PR prattle then making the rounds about a reprised "Boston-Austin axis," as if the new national ticket was auspicious indeed: "Mike is being compared to John F. Kennedy. He is from Massachusetts. He has chosen a running-mate from Texas, and he's going to defeat an incumbent Republican Vice President." As prescient as myth-hawking blather usually is, Carter's statement was part of something much larger than nostalgia for victory in a presidential race. John Kennedy is the archetype for the great Democratic leader taken from us, leaving an empty space yet to be filled.

With impressive cinematic virtuosity, the "JFK" movie—released at the end of 1991—stirred all manner of soupy emotions. Attacked for pretty much all the wrong reasons in the national press and on the airwaves, Oliver Stone's film did have the value of upsetting the most powerful news media; the barrage of "journalistic" assaults on Stone came from the same quarters that had been trying, with no small illogic, to defend the dubious Warren Commission Report since the mid-1960s. But "JFK" the movie tearfully cast JFK the man as the slain incarnation of all that had been good in the political life of the United States. Inflamed with grief and outrage over the murder, "JFK" stoked old fires of passion for one man, as if he had been our true hope for a better tomorrow.

The problem with all the resurgent Kennedy hero-worship was that it had little to do with useful political analysis and much to do with illusions. John Kennedy may (or may not) have been less inclined to escalate the Vietnam War than LBJ turned out to be, and he undoubtedly had made enemies among far-rightists inside and outside the U.S. government. But his presidency was not about aiding the wretched of the earth, it was about crushing them—as can be seen from any realistic look into Kennedy's pet counterinsurgency programs and his vigorous support for U.S. alliances ("for Progress" or whatever) with brutal aristocrats throughout the Third World. Many a peasant organizer and trade union activist in a poor country caught a U.S.-financed bullet in the head during the Kennedy administration before its namesake's own tragic assassination.

The muddled view of United States history as hinging on the personal propensities of presidents may lend itself to standard plot lines of Hollywood and the good ol' two-party system. But why feed such myths? Yes, individuals and their character do matter, in the Oval Office and elsewhere. But the most powerful forces that shape U.S. government policies, foreign and domestic, are geared toward maintaining and extending corporate control, in this country and overseas. Such a real-life plot line may not seem ideal for creating high-tension cinema, but the realities of political power that routinely determine so many lives and deaths are far removed from morality plays about the betrayals of shining princes. Little is gained, and much lost, with mythology asserting that "the people" had the U.S. government in an earlier time and that it was taken from them—as if the country had ever been theirs.

Such false nostalgia feeds current falsity, and passivity, about how substantive change might be created. If a great leader was taken from us, triggering the country's downward trend, then another great man might be just the ticket to set things right. Enter: Bill Clinton.

That Clinton both idolized and imitated JFK was, we can assume, reasonably genuine in addition to being politically shrewd. (The fact that Clinton grew up without Kennedy's privileges of wealth could only sweeten the populist Americana storyline for an Arkansan with a childhood closer to

Tom Sawyer than Little Lord Fauntleroy.) A man in his early twenties preoccupied with maintaining future "political viability" would hardly be oblivious to the advantages of patterning himself after John Kennedy; likening a politician to the martyred president is an ultimate compliment, and it was a comparison that Clinton's aides worked hard to encourage in the media long before he became president. By early 1992 the preferred Clinton mythos was well-established, casting the youthful candidate as JFK: The Next Generation. "The great leaders are great communicators," Clinton's media adviser Frank Greer proclaimed. "And Bill is the best communicator we've had since John F. Kennedy."

Clinton's autumn victory cemented his claim to Kennedy lineage; by then journalists were falling all over each other to conflate old and new legends. "THE TORCH PASSES," declared the headline over *Newsweek*'s lead article—which quickly recalled "a film clip that made its way into a widely seen campaign ad: a beaming, 16-year-old Bill Clinton on a sun-drenched White House lawn, shaking the hand of his and his generation's idol, John F. Kennedy. With Clinton's sweeping victory this week over President George Bush and maverick Ross Perot, the footage rises from mere advertising to the realm of prophetic history. For it documents JFK reaching across the years to a boy he did not know—and to whom the torch of leadership now passes in an emphatic statement of America's desire for change." There was more: "Like Kennedy," Clinton "offered himself as a new kind of youthful, centrist Democrat.... And, like Kennedy, Clinton and his 44-year-old running mate represent a new meritocracy reaching the pinnacle of power."

In the afterglow of Clinton's win, news media were obsessive about a nascent Camelot II. "Now the torch is being passed to the generation that was touched and inspired by Kennedy," *Time* reported. "Indeed, the most memorable moment in the convention video about the man from Hope was the scene of the eager student being inspired by Kennedy's anointing touch." A few weeks later, when *Time* named Clinton "Man of the Year," the cover story began this way: "For years, Americans have been in a kind of vague mourning for something that they sensed they had lost somewhere—what was best in the country, a distinctive American endowment of youth and energy and ideals and luck: the sacred American stuff. They had squandered it, Americans thought, had thrown it away in the messy interval between the assassination of John Kennedy and the wan custodial regime of George Bush." *Time*'s headline: "THE TORCH IS PASSED."

Like his hero, Clinton has a flair for rhetoric that some might hear as pleasantly radical; it was not only that he could call for change, but also that—especially during the '92 fall campaign—he could articulate the necessity of change so insistently. A populist tone is especially important for capturing the White House these days; Carter, Reagan and Clinton all successfully got in by claiming to be "outsiders"; even Perot felt obliged to make such claims, and he took in millions of voters, despite the absurdity of a corporate billionaire posing as just a regular guy. Bill Clinton deftly showed that a politician can win nationwide by accomplishing two key tasks: satisfying elite interests that he will not rock their boats much, while simultaneously satisfying non-elites that he cares about getting them out of the economic swamp they're stuck in. This can be an unbeatable combination, appealing to people wherever they live: A candidate—big on symbols and small on inclination to alter the status quo—is apt to be welcomed for denouncing "greed" and undue deference to the rich, even while serving them.

January 20th of 1993 was an uplifting day. Clinton spoke of forcing a new spring for the nation, and minutes later, from the same spot, Maya Angelou read a moving poem she'd written for the Inauguration. We were to get far better poetry than policy out of the Clinton administration.

"Our presidents at their inaugurals....make us the dupes of our hopes," I.F. Stone wrote a few days into the Nixon administration. Presidents from both parties came in declaring peaceful sentiments, while committed to huge military outlays. "Kennedy proceeded to step up the arms race," Stone recalled, "and Nixon is pledged to do the same."

Bill Clinton was able to take the presidential oath of office because the 1992 Democratic campaign's depiction of G.O.P. villainy had reverberated widely. Telling the public that its concerns were his own, Clinton arrived on the scene to rescue us from the ravages of out-and-out rightist Republican politics—upper-class looting that got out of hand, along with economic torpor and dreadful disregard for the value of human rights. The prospect of going back to a marvelous future could be alluring, even dazzling. (The morning after Clinton won the presidency, I was on the phone with a radio producer for one of California's biggest talk shows, who joyfully exclaimed: "It's going to be like when Jack Kennedy was president!") By late '92, enthusiasm for Clinton often included at least a vague belief in the vision of some sort of second Camelot: belief enhanced by illusions about the first.

On the road seeking political support, John F. Kennedy used pernicious nonsense to fuel momentum for his presidential quest. He repeatedly flayed a bomber gap and a missile gap, both nonexistent. And there were the less renowned whoppers too—as when, in a speech on December 15, 1958, he declared: "I realize that it will always be a cardinal tenet of American foreign policy not to intervene in the internal affairs of other nations—and that this is particularly true in Latin America."

During the early winter of 1960-1961, John Kennedy was careful to consult with venerable foreign-policy officials before moving into the White House; he accepted their world views, and heeded their advice. Blue-blood "national security" elders from the Truman administration, Dean Acheson and Robert Lovett, recommended a fellow named Dean Rusk for secretary of state; and to run the Defense Department, Lovett told Kennedy, the best man would be Robert McNamara.

When it came to staffing the top echelons of Foggy Bottom and the Pentagon, Clinton also deferred to the sensibilities of the wealthy and the wise after his electoral triumph. The preferences of the upper crust were clear. During the early winter of 1992-1993, influential pundits urged Clinton to stick with some familiar policy hands that had steered the ship of state in the past. Soon after the election, *New York Times* columnist Leslie Gelb—himself a former State Department official in the Carter administration—advised Clinton to appoint "a national security team of moderates and conservatives." The rationale was that such appointments would keep hawks from squawking.

Thus was the script played out: A Democrat at last back in the White House—anxious to head off criticism from the right on foreign policy. When it came to facing down the Pentagon establishment, Bill Clinton's presidency was not qualifying as a profile in courage. Christopher Hitchens had it right when he wrote midway through 1993: "The most consistent thing about Clinton, and the thing least noticed about him in a press that swings on the pendulum between sycophancy and bullying, is his surrender of civilian authority to the military-industrial complex."

Ripple effects became apparent stateside in the summer of 1993: Terrified at the prospect of publicly tangling with the Joint Chiefs of Staff, who ostensibly serve at the pleasure of the president, Clinton underscored just how easily his supposed commitments could collapse when he embraced a repressive "don't ask, don't tell, don't pursue" formulation for gay men and lesbians in the armed forces. Even if he'd tried, President Clinton might not have been able to fulfill his campaign promise to lift the ban, given the national firestorm of bigotry that exploded against the idea in early 1993. But the commander-in-chief didn't try.

Instead, he issued a directive that he presented as a real step forward for equal rights within the armed forces. Days later, however, on Capitol Hill, the Defense Department's general counsel testified that Clinton's order involved "no new substantive or procedural rights" for gay people in the military. In essence, the Clinton directive reaffirmed discrimination. "It sends a very strong signal that anti-gay prejudice is still very acceptable," said author Randy Shilts. Gay rights leader Thomas Stoddard asserted that Clinton "acceded, without a fight, to the stereotypes of prejudices he himself had disparaged." David Mixner, a gay activist who'd been a key fundraiser for Clinton during the '92 campaign, was blunt: "No matter how they try to gift wrap this in politic language, it's not a compromise, it's a capitulation."

Eager to gauge which way the winds are blowing, Bill Clinton brokers "compromises" with his presidential finger permanently lifted in the air; it is rare when more than a faint breeze from the left reaches him. We may shrug that a weathervane cannot be held responsible for the political climate, or we may decry an absence of leadership. But people who express warm regard for Clinton's personal attributes are missing the same point as people who vilify him in personal terms: Assumptions about a president's internal integrity or perfidy—star-struck fandom or demonization—distract from the key question. *Whose interests is he serving?*

Clinton may be the least pretentious, most intellectually cogent, and most psychologically healthy president in our lifetime. He may also be among the more craven and cleverly disingenuous when he wants to get out of tight political corners. His personal style may make a difference, but he was in a position to ascend to the presidency in the first place because of alliances he built and functions he proved able to perform. Appreciating or blaming Clinton personally is a waste of energy—and a diversion; our appropriate response is not psychoanalysis but political analysis.

Anyone shocked by Bill Clinton's deference to the nation's powerful after he became president was not paying very close attention beforehand. Clinton became a national figure offering to reconcile the unreconciled. He called for moving beyond "the stale orthodoxies of 'left' and 'right.'" He was verbal and even witty, a humanist without excessive humanism, able to invoke spine-tingling patriotic themes without seeming old-fashioned or hokey or extreme. Most importantly, Clinton was adept at working both sides of a populist street, schmoozing with the money bags and denouncing them as soon as he got across the road.

Lining up with him early on was the chair of the Democratic National Committee, Ron Brown. Inflatable as a mini-myth, blown up just big enough for the purposes at hand, Brown helped preside over the party's convention. (His presence at the podium was ho-hum until a brief adulatory film about him was shown on giant screens to the assembled delegations inside Madison Square Garden; suddenly his reappearance at the rostrum was met with a mighty cheer.) None of the Clinton delegates I talked with that week seemed troubled by Brown's recent history as one of the more reprehensible of Washington lobbyists. As a partner at the Patton, Boggs & Blow law firm—where a computer program matches the interests of corporate donors with the most relevant Congress members looking to raise money—Brown assisted clients including an array of U.S. and foreign business interests, as well as the regime of sadistic Haitian dictator Jean-Claude Duvalier. But concerns about such matters were far away in July 1992. A Democratic victory was in the wind.

II

On a sweltering day just before the 1988 Democratic Convention opened, several thousand people spanned the meadow of an Atlanta park, waiting all humid afternoon for an overdue caravan from Chicago. A choir of black women and men in robes filled the steamy air with one pulsing song after another, part gospel part rock 'n' roll, all spiritual. Then lines of TV cameras aimed toward one side of the stage, where Jesse Jackson, wearing a striped polo shirt, emerged from a swelling mass of people; he turned and pointed thumbs up, beaming to the crowd chanting *Jesse! Jesse!* On stage, he spoke, and I took notes: "We the people must keep hope alive... The pain of a hungry baby... Whether white, black or brown—hunger hurts... Those who want the human race and not the nuclear race... We want a democracy of the many and not the aristocracy of the few... All blood is royal blood... It's so basic. We want to share... Hold on. Don't surrender your dreams..."

Across town at the convention the open ardor of Jackson delegates made party regulars seem, in contrast, like accountants using words that came out as calculations, their emotions displayed flat as spreadsheets. The prevailing pragmatism—swinging on the jambs of power that was personal, economic, political—depended on purveyed myths for the country at large, myths that served as spoonfuls of sugar to help the bromides go down, keeping them palatable, digestible, habit-forming. No acceptance speech could mention, much less set out to confront, the extent of racism and class inequities in everyday national life. (Dukakis had been saying there could be only one quarterback, and Jackson had been saying that cotton pickers should have a role in deciding how rewards get divided in the big house; one man was playing football, the other was tracing legacies from before the Civil War.)

For some, the 1988 convention seemed to be progress—the number of black delegates was at an all-time high, 23 percent—and the tone that permeated the convention hall's sound system and video screens was self-congratulatory: moving pictures of triumphs, then brave, now safe and in the can, glory days of civil rights struggles a quarter-century old. The venerated footage was being shown largely as a substitute for living in the present. Little was offered for someone residing in a neighborhood battle-zone where people kept falling, later added up as statistics; malnutrition, untreated diseases and unemployment could be quantified in numbers, but despair and anger and desperation were too visceral to be easily empirical, too deep for the surface skimming operation of running the national party.

In labyrinths of Atlanta's "World Congress Center" hosting the convention were hordes of journalists, delegates, campaign workers—flushed with importance. Meanwhile other eyes, throughout the massive edifice, watched and blinked and kept watching, unnoticed, part of the backdrop: black service workers, enormous Jesse Jackson buttons nearly the size of teacups pinned to their clothes with pride that was palpable, and silent; they had no standing at this convention, no credentials except the ones that permitted them to scrub the urinals and toilet bowls and sinks. At the end of the week, in front of the ornate facades of glassy hotels, delegations said good-byes next to taxis and airport shuttles, while at the convention complex, banners and displays were coming down with the help of black women inside white-weave service uniforms, "Jackson '88 Keep Hope Alive" saucers still pinned on their gauzy blouses, mutely defying the convention's verdict. Any number of blues songs told of a train always gone, rear lights fading from view; the past few days added to memory another rickety whistle-stop platform, a blood-red sun sinking into dim routine. The day had not come when all the false dawns would be supplanted by one more real.

III

Four years later, when the 1992 Democratic National Convention formally nominated its presidential candidate, one journalist in the press gallery had a special reason to feel excitement. If any book had served as a theoretical blueprint for Bill Clinton's primary campaigns, it was reporter E.J. Dionne's *Why Americans Hate Politics.* The book appeared in early 1991 with adulatory endorsements on the cover from media heavies Mark Shields, Cokie Roberts, William Schneider and Lesley Stahl. But, as it turned out, the most important fan of the book was the governor of Arkansas, trying to hone his message out on the hustings as he spoke to Democratic Party leaders in state after state. By late spring '91, Clinton was praising Dionne as a "very gifted political writer" and crediting him for a frequent catch-phrase in Clinton's speeches—"false choices."

Bill Clinton was eager to reap the benefits of Dionne's analysis, which argued that Democrats and Republicans were stuck in a bad rut of presenting "false choices" to the electorate. The claim had some truth, and even more practical utility for a presidential campaign in 1992. Dionne advised dumping the old liberal-versus-conservative rhetoric, appealing instead to most people's common interests—though as a practical matter that would mean melding the rhetoric of both major parties. For a Democrat eager to capture center ground, Dionne's book offered a political diagram for dodging the "liberal" label without seeming unprincipled. Critiquing "false choices" had the potential to sound visionary rather than expedient, down-to-earth instead of abstract, content-driven instead of ideology-driven. In Dionne's words, "liberalism and conservatism are framing political issues as a series of false choices.... On issue after issue, there is consensus on where the country should move or at least on what we should be arguing about; liberalism and conservatism make it impossible for that consensus to express itself."

Dionne, like Clinton, did not hesitate to place "the middle class"—a euphemism for white and not poor—at the center of the most important political calculus. In contrast, poor people—including millions of blacks and Latinos trapped in urban dead-ends—were peripheral to the New Democrat vision. Their overwhelmingly Democratic votes were predictable (though their election-day turnout was likely to be low, unless they had cause to feel a big stake in the outcome). The "middle class," on the other hand, was up for grabs.

Why Americans Hate Politics suggested painting a political bull's-eye on a majoritarian constituency—alternately referred to as the "broad middle class," "America's restive middle class," and "the restive majority, the great American middle." E.J. Dionne urged politicians to develop "a new politics of the middle class, an approach that represents the ideals and interests of the great mass of Americans in the political and economic center." This "new political center" would be avowedly inclusionary; between the lines, it would also be quite *ex*clusionary. (People beneath the targeted "middle class" would get much less solicitude.) Dionne presented his formula as eclectic ingenuity and not mere pragmatism; yet for a national politician, the resulting equation was liable to produce quite utilitarian graphs, maybe apropos for maximizing chances of a win in the Electoral College.

While insisting that 1990s politics should not mirror exploitative economic setups (which Dionne dubbed "Eighties Right"), the book also maintained that politics should not hammer very hard in the opposite direction ("Sixties Left"); instead of a mirror or a hammer, Dionne's book proposed—in effect—a blender suitable for serving up policy purée. After all, in his words, "voters increasingly look for ways to protest the status quo without risking too much change." Stripped of its unctuous language harkening back to democratic civility that never was, Dionne's book entered a plea for gussying up U.S.

centrism as something new and different.

When Clinton implemented Dionne's suggestions, he garnered lots of good press—not surprising, with the Fourth Estate largely sharing Dionne's
attitudes. As the country's biggest newsweekly, *Time*
was a good barometer. *October 19, 1992:* "The core
of Clinton's economic vision is distinguishable from
the president's and is perhaps best described as a
call for a We decade; not the old I-am-my-brother's-
keeper brand of traditional Democratic liberalism..."
November 16, 1992: "Clinton's willingness to move
beyond some of the old-time Democratic religion is
auspicious. He has spoken eloquently of the need to
redefine liberalism: the language of entitlements
and rights and special-interest demands, he says,
must give way to talk of responsibilities and
duties.... Combining conservative values such as
responsibility and self-help with liberal ones like tolerance and generosity—which is precisely the
covenant that Clinton proposes—could conquer the
corrosive tactic of making wedge issues out of racial
fears and sexual prejudices." *January 4, 1993:*
"Clinton's campaign, conducted with dignity, with
earnest attention to issues and with an impressive
display of self-possession under fire, served to reha-
bilitate and restore the legitimacy of American politics and thus, prospectively, of government itself. He
has vindicated (at least for a little while) the honor
of a system that has been sinking fast."

Dionne's book includes some useful insights
into how ideological abstractions leave most
Americans cold, in the midst of pressing social
problems that have clear negative consequences in
daily life. But, typically, his polemic against political

orthodoxy is thoroughly orthodox in its automatic assumptions about such matters as U.S. "national security" and the virtues of a corporate-dominated society. Adhering to the well-funded myth that the political center can be an island of common ground safely above a nasty sea of ideology, Dionne sets out in search of this lost isle of Atlantis. Drenched with his own ideological suppositions, Dionne's word-processor sails on.

After citing ample reasons for consternation that Americans hate politics so, Dionne is pleased to inform readers that reassurance can be found close to home. Winding up 350 pages on the meaning of politics, he exclaims: "If you want to know the difference between communist dictatorship and democracy, it is this: In the East, government officials, *free from public pressure*, nearly destroyed the environment; in the West, government officials, *responding to public pressure*, cleaned up the environment. In the East, bureaucrats were the polluters. In the West, bureaucrats—the people at the environmental protection agencies—were the foes of pollution." Dionne got it half right, with critical acuities keenly facing eastward. Meanwhile, back in the USA, there is always a bullish market for tall tales from men in pinstripes. How do you like living in a country where the government has "cleaned up the environment"? And what do you think of political analysis that in 1991 could describe "the people at the environmental protection agencies" as "the foes of pollution"? Makes you catch a glimmer of why Americans hate political reporters who purvey such drivel.

To Dionne, a *Washington Post* staffer searching for rays of light at the end of the polarized political tunnel, congressional discourse in the days just before the Gulf War was a wondrous and all-too-rare triumph of substance. "After years of political game-playing, sound-bite mongering, and just plain foolishness," he wrote, "America's politicians demonstrated that they were, indeed, capable of coming to grips with each other's arguments. It was possible in American politics to debate an issue without questioning the motives of an adversary. It was possible to argue fiercely without leaving the country hopelessly divided." Dionne's delight at the "debate" on Capitol Hill prior to the Gulf War is suggestive of the kind of new national order he seeks.

Imbued with the popular "take back America" spirit, Dionne's book supplies a closing paragraph with an invocation that might appeal to any myth-plying politician (or to Hollywood for that matter, or to vital-centrist Arthur Schlesinger Jr., who wrote a 1991 *Wall Street Journal* column referring to America's slaves as "involuntary immigrants"). "In our efforts to find our way toward a new world role," Dionne concluded, "we would do well to revive what made us a special nation long before we became the world's leading military and economic power—our republican tradition that nurtured free citizens who eagerly embraced the responsibilities and pleasures of self-government." The words are on a fishing expedition for nostalgia about a past that never was. Dionne's (and Clinton's) expressed intentions may be evocative of a better future, but only sand castles are appropriate for building on foundations of myths.

IV

What is *myth* and what is *reality* in mainstream U.S. politics? The question raises another: Is there much difference, as a practical matter? Myths that loom large are "real" whenever they are widely propagated by politicians and mass media speaking from the same lexicon. "When *I* use a word, it means just what I choose it to mean—neither more nor less," Humpty Dumpty informed Alice; when the girl posed a dissenting question, he responded impatiently: "The question is, which is to be master—that's all." The closed loops of language are concentric with closed loops of power.

The most powerful ideologies blend in with everyday social landscape. The prevailing constraints are internalized, automatic judgments about what is possible, practical, reasonable, desirable. Ongoing demands from huge institutions—the weightiest pillars around—become our primers and our points of reference. "The political needs of society become individual needs and aspirations, their satisfaction promotes business and the commonweal, and the whole appears to be the very embodiment of Reason," wrote Herbert Marcuse. "And yet this society is irrational as a whole. Its productivity is destructive of the free development of human needs and faculties, its peace maintained by the constant threat of war, its growth dependent on the repression of the real possibilities for pacifying the struggle for existence—individual, national, and international.... The capabilities (intellectual and material) of contemporary society are immeasurably greater than ever before—which means that the scope of society's domination over the individual is immeasurably greater than ever before."

In countries ruled by heavy-handed tyrants, public expression of opposing views may not be allowed at all. Words are thick doors of perception already slammed shut and bolted, so that—in the words of French social critic Roland Barthes—"there is no longer any delay between the naming and the judgment, and the closing of the language is complete."

But the United States is not ruled by tyrants. We enjoy important freedoms—for the most part won with enormous human efforts and many casualties along the way. Our tangible freedoms are precious, yet far less (inherently) empowering than they're cracked up to be. The First Amendment is a good example. A.J. Liebling's famous remark—"freedom of the press is guaranteed only to those who own one"—could be supplemented with an even more ominous conclusion: those who don't own the media are subjugated by those who do. Mass communications and government can reject proposals before the public hears them; our social possibilities are foreclosed before glimpsed, like shuttered horizons kept off the mental map and off the public agenda.

Questions that belong together—such as "Who profits?" and "Who suffers?"—are fragmented, too rarely asked in the same breath or pursued with a steady eye on causality. From the vantage point of elites—looking down from huge institutions casting large shadows over our lives and across the planet—our current uses of freedoms are small impediments to their power. Customary political activities, often made to sound earth-shaking, hardly make those elites tremble.

Illusions of freedom get in the way of exploring how we might be able to transform the present into a really different future. Amid constant delusionary babble, the language of choice is key: We are kept preoccupied and even mesmerized by a profusion of prefab "choices"—on store shelves and showroom floors, on cable TV systems, on newsstands, on election ballots—choices we are free to make after the options have been pre-selected for us. (And they call it democracy.)

While reflecting manipulative systems already in place, language also serves as "an instrument of control even where it does not transmit orders but information; where it demands, not obedience but choice, not submission but freedom." In the process, Marcuse added, "This language controls by reducing the linguistic forms and symbols of reflection, abstraction, development, contradiction; by substituting images for concepts. It denies or absorbs the transcendent vocabulary; it does not search for but establishes and imposes truth and falsehood."

At the time, thirty years ago, Marcuse's observations may have seemed to be overstating; now they understate the fusion of enterprises selling us politicians and inanimate products alike: "If the language of politics tends to become that of advertising, thereby bridging the gap between two formerly very different realms of society, then this tendency seems to express the degree to which domination and administration have ceased to be a separate and independent function in the technological society. This does not mean that the power of the professional politicians has decreased. The contrary is the case. The more global the challenge they build up in order to meet it, the more normal the vicinity of total destruction, the greater their freedom from effective popular sovereignty. But their domination has been incorporated into the daily performances and relaxation of the citizens, and the 'symbols' of politics are also those of business, commerce, and fun."

Bill Clinton playing a jazz saxophone may be a pleasing image—whether a campaign performance on the Arsenio Hall show or a commander-in-chief performance on a U.S. military base in South Korea. (Lee Atwater loved to publicly pick up the blues guitar, even as he designed the racist "Willie Horton" television commercials for the Bush-Quayle ticket in 1988.) The diversionary photo-ops of politics, simultaneously decried and fed by mass media, are in sync with contradictory images we have of ourselves: Most people believe that most people are influenced by TV commercials, but most people contend that they are not among those people.

The "marketplace of ideas" is supposed to be an ennobling concept; yet the phrase itself, meant to be reassuring, is a demeaning fraud—as if genuine ideas can be offered and considered in roughly the same way as new cars and frozen foods. The heavily promoted "ideas" are standardized building materials—for mass-produced structures of belief, acceptance and accommodation—designed to snap together like Lego blocks. The marketplace of ideas has been walling off ideas for a long time.

Four

Long Winding Road

For many kids in the huge baby-boom generation, fresh housing tracts may have had a cookie-cutter appearance, but they offered some real delights, and were part of the only childhood we would ever know. It was a time of expectations and of myths writ large, with frequent self-adulation segueing neatly into Disney TV show heroes and a panoply of other mass-marketed icons as the '50s went on. The intensive circumscribed kaleidoscope that dominated our living rooms was powerful.

On network TV with new episodes from 1954 to 1960, "Father Knows Best" was one of the leading televised family models as boomers grew up. The program's gentle humor and mild pathos enabled the Andersons to overcome difficulties with endearing grace. Now it is nostalgia and camp, but then "Father Knows Best" was immediate, visceral, and formative for millions of kids and quite a few parents. "I'm ashamed I had any part of it," Billy Gray—the actor who played Bud—told an interviewer two decades later. "People felt warmly about the show and that show did everybody a disservice. Hundreds of kids—hundreds—have come up to me and said, 'I really got raked over the coals because of you. My mother keeps asking me why I wasn't like Bud.' I feel responsible to some degree for that. I felt that the show purported to be real life, and it wasn't. I regret that it was ever presented as a model to live by." Gray commented about the "Father Knows Best" cast: "I think we were all well motivated but what we did was run a hoax. We weren't trying to, but that is what it was. Just a hoax."

Meanwhile, away from the scripted TV dramas, a crisis of national conscience was accelerating, as civil rights activists confronted white supremacy in the South; many endured savage brutality as they struggled for equal rights, exemplifying the best of the human spirit. Across the country, Caucasians widely assumed that the white edifice was the best thing going, and integration would mean elevation for Negroes. But in the first years of the 1960s, James Baldwin was among the black writers beginning to question the merits of moving into what he called "a burning house." The structures that concerned him were, as much as anything else, psychological. His astute analysis of the psyches of white Americans was in stark contrast to their own assessments.

Overall, we whites seemed fairly enamored with our images of ourselves; disquiet was muted, very much privatized, or fringy, as with beatnik-types and avant-gardes of other stripes, who mattered little in the early '60s mainstream scheme of things. For many white guys, careers were booming along with the tract-home industry. In a lot of families, dad was getting hefty raises. Except for "juvenile delinquents," stubbornly poor people and other such disreputables, we were in the midst of grabbing the modern world by the tail. With discontent mostly kept confidential, white America had never been more flush and full of itself.

There was, of course, some audible moaning along the way, back then, about the uniformity of men in gray flannel suits, but the lure of affluence had a way of serving as a domestic super-weapon, an all-purpose silencer. Meanwhile, science, in the space age, was to be a savior. If the mix of empiricism and religiosity got uneasy at times, rhetoric provided much glue; invocations of NASA and God were common during the early 1960s. At that time, as a country, we were finding out a great deal about outer space and productivity, but relatively little about inner space or the human treatment of human beings.

II

In the mid-1960s the symbol of liberal deference to the Democrat in the Oval Office was Hubert H. Humphrey, a man so brimming with humanitarianism that his eyes often watered. "He matches energy in the right with compassion for the needs of others," Lyndon Johnson said of his pick for vice president on August 26, 1964. Days earlier, HHH had proven his loyalty by helping to quash a challenge from Mississippi civil rights activists who tried to gain representation for blacks at the Democratic National Convention. Unity, for the president-and-party-leader, was at stake.

Coming after the traumas of the Cuban Missile Crisis in autumn 1962 and the assassination of President Kennedy a year later, Lyndon Johnson's election victory in '64 was to have represented the end of apocalyptic fears—thereafter no more needed than LBJ's campaign commercial on TV with the little girl whose future was (mushroom-)clouded by a nuclear-trigger-happy Barry Goldwater. Extremism had been defeated. Like the previous year's Limited Test Ban Treaty that had banned atmospheric nuclear tests, the national repudiation of Goldwater had strengthened sanity in high places.

Yet, even though the nuclear clouds were now being hidden below the surface of the earth (and of our minds), smoke was billowing from urban ghettos of the North, in what was to become a rite of rage for many summers, from Watts to Harlem. Attempts to define race as a regional problem (the South) were failing. The landmark 1964 Civil Rights Act and 1965 Voting Rights Act left unchanged the dire conditions that gave rise to violent upheaval in the cities. There were early portents of discussions about the USA as a "sick society." But any such notion was still confined to the margins. The main political view saw nothing wrong that the National Guard and perhaps a War on Poverty couldn't cure. Our society was not destined to be ill; it was destined to be Great.

Like Jimmy Carter and Bill Clinton after him, Johnson saw that most liberals could be manipulated to stay in line behind a presidential Democrat. And LBJ's rhetoric was quite appealing, for a while anyway. *March 16, 1964:* "I have called for a national war on poverty. Our objective: total victory." *May 28, 1964:* "So I ask you tonight to join me and march along the road to the future, the road that leads to the Great Society, where no child will go unfed and no youngster will go unschooled; where every child has a good teacher and every teacher has good pay, and both have good classrooms; where every human being has dignity and every worker has a job; where education is blind to color and employment is unaware of race; where decency prevails and courage abounds." But, as would be true fifteen and thirty years later, the Democratic president's budget priorities were soon to negate the lovely sound-bites. Hubert Humphrey led the rationalizers—"pragmatists" all, not unlike the Clinton loyalists three decades later—who could not dream of breaking with the Democrat in the White House.

While sending several hundred thousand troops to Vietnam, the Johnson administration stepped up daily bombardment of the countryside across wide areas of Indochina. Official documents, later released by Daniel Ellsberg as "the Pentagon Papers," make clear that the U.S. government was uninterested in a peaceful settlement.

As the war escalated, so did the presidential mendacity. *August 10, 1964:* "Our one desire—our one determination—is that the people of Southeast Asia be left in peace to work out their own destinies in their own way." *April 10, 1965:* "We love peace. We hate war. But our course is charted always by the compass of honor." *June 3, 1965:* "The American people want to be a part of no war. But the American people want no part of appeasement or of any aggression." *January 12, 1966:* "We fight for the principle of self-determination, that the people of South Vietnam should be able to choose their own course..." *February 23, 1966:* "Our purpose is solely to defend against aggression." *May 11, 1966:* "Strident emotionalism in the pursuit of truth, no matter how disguised in the language of wisdom, is harmful to public policy, just as harmful as self-right-eousness in the application of power." *May 17, 1966:* "There will be some Nervous Nellies and some who will become frustrated and bothered and break ranks under the strain. And some will turn on their leaders and on their country and on our fighting men."

The most pertinent response came from the streets, from outside the bounds of sanctified discourse. "Realistic" leftish voices warned that denunciation of the incumbent Democratic president would help the Republicans; those voices had to be defied. In April 1967, the first anti-Vietnam-War march in excess of 100,000 people wended through Manhattan to U.N. Plaza, where Martin Luther King Jr. and others denounced the war as illegal and immoral. Inch by inch, the near-consensus behind the war's buildup was unraveling. Yet, in 1967, to publicly oppose the war invited avalanches of ridicule and vilification.

Dissent grew. More of us North American boomers started to believe that we were part of a great leapfrog forward; necessity demanded that we be lithe, audacious and unattached to the past, however recent. Feeling unbound by history had its benefits (however temporary), and so did the blending of New Left and hippie sensibilities. More than a few flowers, inserted by anti-war protesters, were photographed in the barrels of rifles held by members of the U.S. armed forces.

Naïveté and brilliance tended to overlap in a peace-movement milieu that was inclined to turn mystical as convenience dictated. For a time, the melding of any number of thought streams could work just dandy—we could throw the cultural kitchen sink at the $y$tem and screw it up royally. There need be no serious contradiction between Timothy Leary and Herbert Marcuse, Ho Chi Minh and Hermann Hesse, Che and Siddharta, Watts (Alan) and Watts (California), Marx (Karl) and Marx (Groucho). Drug-bridged eclecticism seemed to work as a tactic against the American establishment.

According to that establishment's script, the intellect—rational and increasingly civilized—was to determine human activity; any discomfort along the concrete road was to be accepted as part of the regimen of the affluent society. But young intellects began to notice less linear cornucopias, yielding sensory delights and psychological exploration, as marijuana wafted in the air; the intellect could not do much to reconcile such pleasures with rigid mid-1960s social norms and the moral postures of U.S. officials who kept exhorting support for warfare against Vietnam. "Make love Not war" was more than syncopated rhetoric; it was a concise statement of preference, an attempted solicitation and injunction. First a few, and then more, and then millions of American kids reached out for the balm that Flower Power offered.

To take one's own feelings seriously, to place them above the edicts of authorities and to act on this new sense of priorities—the world was opening; pot and psychedelic drugs helped loosen the strictures of social straightjackets while new winds of music, clothes, politics, language swept through hair like the flowers in Scott McKenzie's sparkling ode to San Francisco and the Summer of Love. In 1967 the underground went over the top, waves upon waves in nonviolent assault for our senses and against the rigidity of a dominant society in the United States.

"In this place, and more particularly, in this time, generations appear to flower, flourish, and wither with the speed of light," James Baldwin wrote. He added:

> The flower children were all up and down the Haight-Ashbury section of San Francisco—and they might have been everywhere else, too, but for the vigilance of the cops—with their long hair, their beads, their robes, their fancied resistance, and, in spite of a shrewd, hard skepticism as unnerving as it was unanswerable, really tormented by the hope of love.... Their flowers had the validity, at least, of existing in direct challenge to the romance of the gun; their gentleness, however specious, was nevertheless a direct repudiation of the American adoration of violence. Yet they looked—alas—doomed. They seemed to sense their doom. They really were flower children, having opted out on the promises and possibilities offered them by the shining and now visibly perishing republic. I could not help feeling, watching them, knowing them to be idealistic, fragmented, and impotent, that, exactly as the Third Reich had had first to conquer the German opposition before getting around to the Jews, and then the rest of Europe, my republic, which, unhappily, I was beginning to think of as the Fourth Reich, would be forced to plow under the flower children—in all their variations—before getting around to the blacks and then the rest of the world.
> ....
>
> The flower children....were in the streets in the hope of becoming whole. They had taken the

first step—they had said, No. Whether or not they would be able to take the second step, the harder step—of saying, Yes, and then going for their own most private broke—was a question which much exercised my mind, as indeed it seemed to exercise the minds, very loosely speaking, of all the tourists and policemen in the area.... [T]he eyes that watched seemed to feel that the children were deliberately giving away family secrets in the hope of egging on the blacks to destroy the family. And that is precisely what they *were* doing—helplessly, unconsciously, out of a profound desire to be saved, to live. But the blacks already knew the family secrets and had no interest in them. Nor did they have much confidence in these troubled white boys and girls. The black trouble was of a different order, and blacks had to be concerned with much more than their own private happiness or unhappiness. They had to be aware that this troubled white person might suddenly decide not to be in trouble and go home—and when he went home, he would be the enemy.

In the years that followed, many hippies and political dissenters did go home, one way or another, to relative comfort and security. Social "assets" and safety nets, such as white skin and some measure of affluent upbringing or academic access, could stand them in good stead. It's true that rebels were apt to encounter harsh treatment from police and courts (as usual, crackdowns were harsher against blacks and Latinos and Native Americans), but as time went on, financial stresses and inducements would prove more powerful than overt repression in getting many fledgling leftists to straighten up and fly right, or at least closer to the center.

Yet, in the meantime, much was gained from breakthroughs large and small, social and intimate, in the course of a few tumultuous years. Across the country, some cohesive momentum emerged to resist deadly assumptions. One of the most vital of the spreading realizations was that authenticity would not—could not—be bestowed from above; it had to be sought and lived, personally and collectively. Over a period of a few years, millions of people (including a sizeable minority of the USA's baby boomers) participated in a life-affirming new kaleidoscope of energy that encompassed countless demonstrations for peace and social justice.

Certainly "the movement" in the 1960s had many flaws, some serious: As per their conditioning, males were often arrogant and oppressive toward females, with sexism the routine order of the day; whites inordinately dominated many organizations that should have had multiracial leadership; concerns among white and affluent constituencies too often overshadowed issues affecting the daily lives of the poor and racial minorities; by 1968 portions of the New Left were tangled up in Leninist rhetoric and facile romanticization of "picking up the gun"; flighty and superficial participation existed side-by-side with deep and lasting commitment. Even at its best—times of the most inclusive and assertive non-violent protest—the movement did not actively involve most boomers, let alone most Americans. Yet the achievements were many, and creative ferment in the air blended counterculture with political resistance: an explosive combustion of opening minds, music, sensuality, and direct action.

If saying No to a grim itinerary is far easier than

saying Yes to an arduous quest for "becoming whole," then drugs are much more useful for the easy part. In the late '60s, drugs were supposed to provide short-cuts...but unfortunately, even in the middle run, life doesn't shortcut too well. Even the best drugs, like marijuana or psilocybin, could easily turn out to be accompanying us along a rocky road paralleling the established highways. It should have been obvious that drugs had no inherent political or ethical qualities (stupid claims by the likes of Timothy Leary notwithstanding). A soldier could smoke pot or drop LSD and throw grenades into peasant villages; a stockbroker could trip out on ticker-tape. Yet it was tempting to fantasize that a drug could somehow counteract the leverage of the power structure.

Like the idealized lawns in the new suburban tracts and the old home towns, our minds were supposed to stay carefully trimmed and edged. A lot of mental energy went into setting aside feelings. For many who were adolescents or young adults a quarter of a century ago, the clash of cerebral and emotional reactions became crucial back then. The battle fought inside many of us—and within family after family and school after school—centered on what to do with unauthorized feelings. At the outset they had, in most situations, virtually no place to go. When we discovered ways to express them, we found that the everyday world around us could undergo drastic change.

In 1967 a classmate of mine printed up and distributed a leaflet—headlined "Napalm A Dog?"—in which he announced that he would be burning a dog on the high school's front steps as a protest of the Vietnam War; the ensuing uproar was such that he got expelled, partially with the rationale that any number of students couldn't wait to beat him up. Living perhaps a dozen miles from the White House, he had done something scurrilous, almost kamikaze-like, in a social context where it was fine to napalm human beings but not canines; the drastic measure of expulsion (a suburban testament to grievous sin) was an index of his foolhardiness.

III

Turning and turning in the widening gyre
The falcon cannot hear the falconer;
Things fall apart; the center cannot hold;
Mere anarchy is loosed upon the world,
The blood-dimmed tide is loosed, and everywhere
The ceremony of innocence is drowned;
The best lack all conviction, while the worst
Are full of passionate intensity.

It was logical that more than one pundit would find in W.B. Yeats' lines some coherent dismay applicable to the late '60s. But in the long run, however fraught with corruptions and contradictions, the center could hold. "The Man Can't Bust Our Music," a record-company ad declared, but much that accompanied the passage of time could. Institutions with status-quo agendas could fall back on vast material resources, continuity, and staying power. "The center" had a way of reasserting itself. For many, what became remembered as "the '60s" lasted only a few seasons. It was, measured against a lifetime, not much longer than a memorable storm punctuating the course of a year. Yet the changes were often searing, and even if shrugged off they left their birthmarks and scars.

We kept getting older, of course, but much more was at work. We were backtracking after too many short-cuts, taken in a frenetic time that encouraged its share of sloppy conceits: such as notions that one's upbringing could be discarded, and various other cultures could be tried on, like hats stocked on department store shelves. For a while it was pleasant to believe that we had changed irreversibly, and almost effortlessly, turning away from craven conformity and cold comforts; but time would tell. We were all part of a continuum of history, social environment, personal foibles, economic conditions—the obvious—which wasn't terribly obvious in the midst of all that '60s commotion. A mindset of insurrection could be a good weapon against a numbed culture, but not necessarily much of a basis for constructing something different.

We could define ourselves in terms of what we weren't. It was more difficult to even begin to create who and what we wanted to be. It was easier to step away from the usual, the abhorrent, the predictable, than to plunge toward a far more wispy future. Options worthy only of contemptuous rejection were everywhere; the questions we might be enthusiastic about answering in the affirmative were just starting to be asked.

Decades as epochs are commonly more hype than real dividing lines. Yet, it turned out that transitions between the '60s and '70s were fairly brusque. Certain intensities seemed to peak at around the same time. A conspicuous shared experience came in the spring of 1970: The U.S. invasion of Cambodia had hardly begun when the peace movement responded with an outpouring of protest across America. Tear gas was the national analgesic. Bullets from law-enforcement troops killed six students, at Kent State in Ohio and Jackson State in Mississippi. Suddenly, in early May, the Pentagon death-merchants were on the defensive. Hundreds of campuses shut down entirely, except for demonstrations; hundreds more went through stages of paralysis. There would, it seemed, be no turning back. And yet, when autumn came, the campuses opened with little more than a murmur. Maybe we had reached our limits, collectively and personally— the exact sequence could be more than a little murky. Additional years of the Vietnam War followed, along with less cohesive opposition at home.

Even when anti-war protests surged, the mass media downplayed their importance. In 1971, when May Day demonstrations in Washington resulted in thousands of arrests, news coverage was sensationalistic and fleeting, with little mention of the life-and-death reasons behind the large-scale civil disobedience. Increasingly, many peace advocates put energy into the campaign of Democratic presidential candidate George McGovern; yet an independent anti-war movement kept asserting itself.

At the Republican National Convention in August 1972, as Richard Nixon was being renominated for president in Miami, several thousand people were in the streets outside, day after day, protesting the still-horrendous Vietnam War. I remember Daniel Ellsberg saying, "We are not on the wrong side in Vietnam. We *are* the wrong side."

Long Winding Road

Dave Dellinger, in the midst of a long fast, read from a letter smuggled out of a Nazi concentration camp three decades earlier—"It was hard at first, but we got used to it." Referring to present-day destruction of so many people in Indochina, Dellinger said: "Although it was hard at first, there is a real possibility we will get used to it." *There is; we have,* I wrote in my journal. After mace and tear gas, more than 900 people were arrested for civil disobedience; but the mass media ignored us. Times had changed.

In 1968, the news coverage had been immense when anti-war protests filled the streets of Chicago as that city hosted the Democratic National Convention; violent attacks on protesters by club-wielding police angered some of the viewers who saw the bloodshed on nationwide TV. In 1972, Danny Schechter observed in a *Boston Phoenix* article: "More demonstrators turned out in Miami this year than in Chicago four years ago. Almost twice as many ended up getting arrested. The demonstrations themselves represented a much more diverse group of people, and many of the protests were among the more creative in conception. Only this time when the 'whole world was watching,' they saw the imported youth galleries chanting, 'four more years' rather than the photographs of Vietnamese horror being carried in the streets. In their post-mortems, the television commentators assured their audiences that the protest movement had had its last hurrah.... Few of the activists were interviewed; little of what they had written or said was reported or taken seriously.... The banal and insulting coverage accorded the anti-war movement in Miami suggests that television can no longer be relied on, if ever it could, as even an unconscious ally."

By 1972, anti-war sentiment was widespread but somehow diffuse, and largely discounted. News media promulgated the idea that the movement had collapsed.

IV

During the 1970s, numerous alternative institutions dug in, or evolved, or got started, for the long haul; people organized projects ranging from listener-supported radio stations to food coops to credit unions to activism on a wide variety of political issues. Yet many other individuals and groups fell by the wayside; in the long run, many of the holes punched in retaining walls of duplicity were patched up and smoothed over.

The trend among many baby boomers could be partly explained by economic concerns. By the mid-1970s, meeting basic expenses required appreciably more income—and there was little money to be made outside the mainstream. Yet all we'd ever had was daily life; if much of it was taken up, yet again, with doing things we didn't particularly want to do, going through motions of being who we didn't particularly want to be, in some senses our lives were slipping away.

After exploring some depths, many people felt constrained to return to the surface, like explorational divers who'd tired of the pressure and risk. As "the '60s" became memory, large numbers of those who'd identified with the counterculture, apolitical or not, gravitated to some form of me-first ideology—with their lives, if not with their mouths— often bent on chasing lots of dollars. There were careers to be built, families to be raised, and money to be made. The danger was that, perhaps in imperceptible increments, we would become a new generation's version of the people we'd warned ourselves against.

As the Vietnam War and the Watergate scandal wound down, the system was pleased to portray both as aberrant incidents that had unduly roused us from serenity. "Our long national nightmare is over," Gerald Ford proclaimed when sworn in as president after Richard Nixon's resignation on August 9, 1974. By then few U.S. troops remained in Vietnam, though the Pentagon was still assisting with the savage "Vietnamization" of the war. When Saigon fell the following year, the war was "over"— though people across Indochina were left to mourn dead loved ones numbering into the millions, and to cope with ecological disasters such as dioxin-poisoning that the American "protectors" had left behind. In the United States, the misapprehension that the Vietnam War had been some kind of aberration from the system (rather than a particularly murderous manifestation of it) was well expressed by a taunt aimed at former peace activists: "Now that the war is over, they won't have anything to protest."

As the anti-establishment furor that had rocked the country for several years passed into history, many of its enthusiasts floated back toward the mainstream. Even the most buoyant of activists had to agree by the mid-1970s that the U.S. left was somewhat adrift. A lot of its rhetorical and ideological excesses had dissipated as well, which was generally to the good. But the movement was smaller, or at least less visible and vehement; progressive politics became more scattered, and often more hazy.

In January 1977 a Democrat arrived in the White House who never managed to talk straight about Vietnam; after two months in office, President Carter explained that the United States had no responsibility to provide postwar aid to Vietnam because "the destruction was mutual." True, it could be said that Carter was better than his Republican predecessors. And the former governor—who'd gained national prominence with help from powerful and wealthy patrons—spoke in very moral tones. But contrary to his enduring humanitarian image, burnished by frequent epiphanies for peace and human rights, Jimmy Carter's presidency set in motion a new wave of horrific policies. For instance—to take a few military-related matters—he pushed forward an array of new nuclear weapons systems such as the Trident, MX, cruise and Pershing 2 missiles, scuttled possibilities for a nuclear test ban under pressure from the weapons labs, and boosted the Pentagon budget at the expense of domestic social programs.

The warm feelings that many humanistic people expressed about Jimmy Carter while he was president—and still express today—reflect the kind of tenacious illusions that now prettify perceptions of President Clinton. Relief at the departure of Republicans from the White House encourages rosy visions as an idealistic-sounding Democrat settles in. All too often, the public-relations image makes a lasting impression that overrides the grimmer realities of presidential policy.

Long Winding Road

Lovely speeches aside, Jimmy Carter opted for guns over butter. His 1976 campaign pledged to expand social programs; instead, during the Carter presidency, the federal spending for them had a growth rate of 4 percent, compared with 8 percent during the Nixon and Ford years. "The Carter administration," writes Manning Marable, "halted the creation of new programs in human-services areas; increased defense spending to all-time highs; and vowed to 'cut inflation and to stimulate the business sector' at the cost of higher unemployment." By 1978, President Carter was giving the green light to huge budget increases for the Pentagon—laying out scenarios for new weapons deployments and other military buildups that the Reagan administration later fulfilled with a vengeance.

Meanwhile, despite all his trumpeted emphasis on "human rights," President Carter funneled large amounts of money and military hardware to many a bloodthirsty dictatorship. Indonesia was a case in point. Inaugurated thirteen months after Indonesia's December 1975 invasion of East Timor, Carter ordered a stepup in U.S. military aid to the Jakarta regime, which was continuing its wholesale murder of Timorese civilians; the death toll was to reach an estimated 200,000 by the time Carter began his last year in the White House. "By 1977, Indonesia had actually begun to exhaust its military supplies in this war against a country of 700,000 people," Noam Chomsky recounts, "so the Carter administration took some time off from its pieties and self-acclaim about its devotion to human rights—'the soul of our foreign policy'—to arrange a large-scale increase in the flow of arms to Indonesia, in the certain knowledge that they would be used to consummate a massacre that was approaching genocidal proportions."

How can such a president be remembered with fondness by people in the USA who detested Ronald Reagan and George Bush for their barbarism? Was Jimmy Carter's treatment of Indonesian butchers an isolated instance? Hardly.

Central America was another region that paid in blood. *Consider El Salvador:* Ignoring the pleas of Archbishop Oscar Romero, who—shortly before his assassination in March 1980—beseeched the president not to send U.S. military aid to the brutal Salvadoran junta, Carter gave El Salvador's terrible war its start with major aid and political backing. *Consider Nicaragua:* Popular mythology tells a very different tale, but "Carter supported [dictator Anastasio] Somoza virtually to the end of his bloody rule," Chomsky notes, "with Israel taking over the main burden at the end—surely with tacit U.S. approval despite official denials—when direct U.S. intervention was blocked by congressional human rights legislation." *Consider Guatemala:* "U.S. military aid to the mass murderers never ceased during the Carter years, contrary to what is commonly alleged, and in fact remained close to the norm. Furthermore, the U.S. military establishment maintained its close relations with the Guatemalan military, giving them a 'convincing signal' that the human rights rhetoric was hardly to be taken seriously."

While engaging in various behind-the-scenes cruelties, the Carter presidency coincided with years of wide ambiguity among progressive activists in the United States. For many people who'd found a sense of identity in the social ferment of the '60s, political commitment shrank into ambivalence. Still, some impressive protests took root; for example, a strong movement grew to challenge nuclear power with public education, legal interventions and nonviolent civil disobedience campaigns.

Many baby boomers had been turning inward. Some results of the new introspection could be positive, even (to use a much-abused word) liberating. A "second wave" of feminism during the 1970s raised crucial questions about sex roles and hierarchy—and began to answer them with radical changes in day-to-day life—in the process creating more egalitarian personal relationships and more democratic social groups. Ongoing discussions highlighted the need for women's liberation, gay rights and an end to male domination.

When Edward Kennedy—objecting to White House budget priorities—opted to run for the 1980 Democratic presidential nomination, he didn't get far against the political hardball of the incumbent. The party's center held. One reason Carter could win renomination so easily was that leftists did not despise him as many had learned to hate Johnson or Nixon. (Yet, for people who bothered to find out what was going on in El Salvador during Carter's final year in the Oval Office, for instance, such antipathy could easily develop.) By 1980, the political culture was such that people who'd been young adults ten years earlier were now less inclined to be outraged about brutalities financed by the U.S. Treasury—from the impoverished neighborhood across town to peasant villages many thousands of miles away.

As usual, attempts to build a national electoral base outside the Democratic Party proved to be inauspicious. With some fanfare on the left, the newly formed Citizens Party nominated Barry Commoner to run for president in 1980. Although substantial numbers of activists volunteered, the effort was a miscalculation on at least two fronts: The independent campaign did not generate wider support, and could not break through mass-media censorship.

Yet grassroots organizing gave rise to some successes at the polls. One of the most inspiring campaigns was in Chicago, where extensive community meetings in the city's black neighborhoods developed a detailed political agenda—and drafted Harold Washington as a mayoral candidate to move it forward. Adding to the obstacles posed by the city's powerful Democratic Party machine, Edward Kennedy and Walter Mondale went out of their ways to endorse the white candidates (Jane Byrne and Richard Daly Jr.) backed by local elites in the Democratic primary. When Harold Washington won enough votes to become Chicago's mayor, his victory was a triumph for people power. Elected in 1983 because progressives of all races put together a strong coalition, he served in city hall as an unwavering advocate for justice and human dignity.

V

In the 1980s, new movements emerged to go up against U.S. complicity with oppression overseas. Midway through the decade, civil disobedience at the South African Embassy in Washington inspired effective anti-apartheid organizing in every region of the United States. Thousands of students worked to demand an end to college investments in companies doing business in South Africa; demonstrations led to victories on many campuses. And attention also focused on other vital concerns—among them, events in Central America. Visits to the region helped to create understanding that galvanized growing numbers of people in North America. Intensive solidarity work drew in many thousands, who educated and agitated and protested against continued U.S. aid to the Contra guerrillas in Nicaragua, and to the death-squad government of El Salvador, and to the succession of dictatorships in Guatemala. The activism built alliances with the poor of Central America, and also educated U.S. citizens about their own government.

Awareness also spread about the dangers of nuclear arms. The Reagan administration provoked alarm with notably reckless bluster as it sought to justify going ahead with new nuclear weaponry that had been backed by President Carter. Intensive community organizing and protests at weapons facilities, embryonic during Carter's presidency, leapt forward with rapid momentum in the early 1980s.

At about the time that the anti-nuclear-weapons cause was reaching new heights of national visibility—filling New York's Central Park with a million protesters on June 12, 1982, and splashing onto the covers of national newsweeklies—the Freeze movement took off. It provided hope, based on intellectual and moral suasion: promoting a proposal to freeze U.S. and Soviet nuclear arsenals at existing levels, as a step toward later cutbacks. Respectable, legal, outspoken and persuasive, with an active support base concentrated among the affluent, "the Freeze" made an enormous impact on mass media and on Capitol Hill. Within two years the national leadership of the Freeze and much of its rank-and-file had become adjuncts to the Democratic Party and its 1984 presidential candidate, Walter Mondale.

The former vice president was a fitting champion of pro-Freeze partisans fighting hard for Pyrrhic achievements at the polls. Eighteen months before he gained the '84 Democratic nomination for president, I phoned Mondale's office and requested an interview with someone authorized to speak for him on the subject of nuclear weapons policies; I was referred to an executive at one of the major stock brokerage firms on Wall Street.

What happened in 1984 was a classic instance of how top Democrats can get activists to accept an absence of clarity and truthfulness (attributes that distinguish an empowered movement from powerful politicians). Mondale was pleased to claim, as he did after one of his primary victories, that when citizens cast ballots for him "they voted to end this insane arms race, so that our children can have a future." In reality, a vote for Mondale represented nothing of the kind; he favored every new nuclear weapons system coming down the pike.

A few weeks before the '84 Democratic national convention, I wrote in an article that Mondale's support for the Freeze was "more fig leaf than litmus test," and commented: "To a remarkable degree, the country's groundswell against nuclear weapons has been willing to project its own hopes onto whoever the Democrats nominate." Soon after the piece appeared in a daily newspaper in California, I received an angry note from the director of one of the main anti-weapons lobbying groups in Washington; he did not dispute the truth of what I'd written about Mondale, but insisted that it should not be put into print. Articles like mine, he complained, would harm efforts to defeat Reagan. A few months later, in his final debate with President Reagan, Mondale assured the country: "I support the air-launched cruise missile, ground-launched missile, Pershing missile, the Trident submarine, the D-5 submarine, the Stealth technology, the Midgetman—we have a whole range of technology."

Was it wrong to urge people to vote for Mondale as a way of preventing Reagan's re-election? Not really. Was it wrong to portray Mondale as an opponent of nuclear madness? Absolutely. Whether or not Mondale went on to win the election, such duplicity by nuclear-freeze strategists could only be catastrophic for the grassroots movement against nuclear weapons. The Freeze handed its momentum and stature over to the 1984 Democratic ticket, which was pleased to squander the gift for electoral purposes. And so the nationwide Freeze movement was strangled by its compacts with Democratic Party tacticians. In the name of fueling hope, fervent hopes were replaced with false ones. When the national Freeze organization and its allies put forward the Democratic Party's liberal politicians as engines for nuclear disarmament, much of the anti-nuclear movement was pulled off track. In the wake of the '84 election, the national Freeze and many other segments of the anti-nuclear movement were buried in the wreckage.

A few hours after the polls closed for the 1984 election, I wrote a piece that tried to sort out what had happened in the Freeze movement's dance with the Democratic Party's presidential campaign: "In the person of Walter Mondale, millions of Americans voted for—and many worked for—someone backing weaponry they detest. The logic, of course, was to defeat an even more repugnant candidate. But by now much of the language accompanying freeze advocacy has been so trivialized that the disarmament constituency is likely to find it more of an encumbrance than a boost in the future. There is something to the old adage about saying what we mean and meaning what we say. In the long run such an approach—while running the risk of appearing naïve—avoids a far graver risk: outmaneuvering our own deeper beliefs. At best, sought-after victories, if won, might truly be weighty victories instead of hollow ones, of the sort that litter the nuclear age landscape of 'arms control'.... Paradoxically, what has seemed to be the 'nuclear freeze' concept's strongest feature—a broad base of support—has circumscribed its possibilities. Wide but not deep, in the end the freeze was not anchored much of anywhere."

Four years later, at the Democratic National Convention in Atlanta, there was a pathetic post-script: Two of the darlings of the Freeze—Senator Alan Cranston and Representative Edward Markey—were hauled out by the Michael Dukakis campaign to speak *against* a minority platform plank (offered by Jesse Jackson delegates) calling for the U.S. government to pledge no-first-use of nuclear weapons in any future conflict. Often lionized earlier in the decade as heroic Freeze advocates, the pair of liberals delivered their well-placed kicks from the podium. The minority plank went down to defeat.

The Reagan administration and right-wing media did not undermine the movement against nuclear weapons. Liberal politicians and mainstream media did—to the great extent that activists trusted them. Eager to heed the advice from friendly voices in Congress and the nation's newsrooms, all too many activist groups deferred to moderating influences. The pattern was customary: What looked like pragmatism turned out to be co-option, greased by mass media.

Five

The Politics
of News Media

In *1984* George Orwell wrote about the conditioned reflex of "stopping short, as though by instinct, at the threshold of any dangerous thought. It includes the power of not grasping analogies, of failing to perceive logical errors, of misunderstanding the simplest arguments if they are inimical" to the prevailing ideology, "and of being bored or repelled by any train of thought which is capable of leading in a heretical direction."

Today's dominant news media are good at repeatedly covering the same ground, carefully avoiding much exploration beyond the sanctioned boundaries. A narrow band of terrain is trod as if it were the universe of ideas. We may get used to equating what is familiar with what is "objective"; what is usual with what is balanced; what is repeatedly asserted with what is true. All the while, enthroned pundits fill the airwaves with nonstop droning that offers little diversity. As with broadcasts, so with print: Newsstands display dozens of papers and magazines, endlessly repetitious and confined.

Words, language, dialogue and debate are potential tools for breaking out of small conceptual cages. But after the thousands of times that Americans have heard the word "freedom" in speeches and sound-bites and TV commercials, for instance, how much meaning can the word hold? In a hollow din, when the mouthing of words has become a self-referencing closed loop of verbiage, words commonly precede—and preempt—thought. When words supplant meaning, clichés become its impersonator and its frequent enemy. In *1984,* Orwell explained that "the special function of certain Newspeak words...was not so much to express meanings as to destroy them." Repetition of such words and phrases can be much like water on stone—constant media drips presenting self-evident truths—courtesy of government officials and the journalists, commentators, academics and assorted other experts who seem to have tenure on the networks.

Serving as a central(ized) nervous system of the country's body politic, U.S. mass media have paralyzing effects. The more ubiquitous that media power becomes, the more anonymous and natural it is likely to seem. Common preconceptions are mistaken for common sense. Even "controversial" news stories are respectful of limitations; the standard paradigm is to bemoan various ills while omitting specifics about causality.

Countless stories describe homelessness but not the real-estate maneuvers connected to it; daily newspapers don't print photos of the profiteers next to the pictures of their victims. Even when journalists focus sharply on the effects of pollution, the extent of the profitable corporate arrogance involved rarely gets into the media frame. And discussions of alternatives stay quite limited: Don't hold your breath for the day when the op-ed page of the *New York Times* or *Washington Post* hosts a vigorous debate about the merits of cutting the Pentagon budget in half next year, or putting a legal cap on the profits of corporations and the assets of millionaires, or holding free elections in each workplace to select supervisors and CEOs. Many democratic possibilities are automatically beyond the pale of mass-media discussion.

Fortunately, even the most powerful manipulators can't be sure of controlling minds. Yet powers-that-be are much more concerned with actions and utterances than with thoughts or feelings per se. And expression of stray dissenting opinions can be tolerated, perhaps even encouraged—letting off steam while the pressure-cooker remains sealed fairly tight. Successful manipulation plays the percentages among the populace, and commands majorities.

The process is even more powerful than the content. Mass media cajole people to keep buying products as if they could substitute for—or even *be*—meaning. "There is, of course, no reason why the new totalitarianisms should resemble the old," Aldous Huxley foresaw in his postwar introduction to *Brave New World.* He added: "A really efficient totalitarian state would be one in which the all-powerful executive of political bosses and their army of managers control a population of slaves who do not have to be coerced, because they love their servitude. To make them love it is the task assigned, in present-day totalitarian states, to ministries of propaganda, newspaper editors and schoolteachers.

But their methods are still crude and unscientific."
That was in 1946. Methods are quite a bit less
crude now.

II

More and more, a brazen new world blends
pacification and repression in a warlock's brew
stirred with both carrot and stick. Mass-produced
seductions combine with mass-imposed intimida-
tions. But whatever the mix of caressing or blud-
geoning people into submission, any effective system of control must go a long way toward obscuring
key methods of that control. A society's vaunted
"stability" (amid chronic and extreme inequities)
may be an index of just how numbed people have
become; in this, the most scientific of ages, people
are beset by social engineering that has come to
seem normal, even natural. This is not a drum-tight
Big Brother society (although U.S. elites have helped
to sustain regimes in quite a few Third World countries as brutal as anything described in *1984*). Some
Americans are apt to feel as carefree as any soma-
swallower. Yet others—such as many inner-city residents overwhelmed by the system—are as desperate as Winston contemplating the grip of Big
Brother.

In the United States, centralization of mass
media is so intrinsic and so crucial that it is not—
must not be—discussed in any discerning way via
the main media channels that empty into our lives
like so much tap water. How many corporations are
reaping most of the revenue from U.S. newspapers,
magazines, TV, books and movies? In the early
1980s the answer was *fifty;* by the early 1990s the

number had dropped to *twenty*. All the pretensions aside, we will not hear Dan Rather or Peter Jennings or Tom Brokaw elucidate how the corporations that pay their salaries are wielding power in pursuit of the bottom line, close to home and around the world.

On millions of TV screens at any one moment, CNN Headline News keeps splattering the country—and the planet—with its jejune ejaculations. Welcome to the global pillage. The technology is awesome, and so is its proven capacity to entrance while conflating actual events with fabricated images, the most pseudo of "realities." During the Gulf War, the media acclaim was widespread when CNN aired live video of U.S. cruise missiles reaching Baghdad; yet what we saw on television was little more than a light show—spectacular pyrotechnics in the sky while the carnage below got short shrift. In the closing decade of the 20th century, the media powers have global reach.

Meanwhile: Criticism is surrounded and absorbed, amoeba-like, by the circuitous mainstreams of what we could call "skipthought"—repeating and recycling endlessly. Skipthought habitually jumps over ideas and perspectives that reject the legitimacy of corporate rule. Elsewhere, in places as far away as East Timor or Turkey or China or Burma, rank lies and flagrant violence may hammer human beings from dawn to dawn, but here and now in the United States the lies and violence are apt to be combined with soothing velvet that adorns the dominant scenery. The biggest hoaxes depend on the biggest illusions. Wholesale, they make the reigning "freedom" possible.

FALSE HOPE

The USA's major news media pose no threat to what the late writer Walter Karp called *the fact of oligarchy*. In the United States, he pointed out, "the fact of oligarchy is the most dreaded knowledge of all, and our news keeps that knowledge from us. By their subjugation of the press, the political powers in America have conferred on themselves the greatest of political blessings—Gyges' ring of invisibility. And they have left the American people more deeply baffled by their own country's politics than any people on earth. Our public realm lies steeped in twilight, and we call that twilight news."

Journalists are neither more nor less courageous than people in other professions; we can hardly expect corporate-paid reporters and pundits to make careers out of biting the hands that sign their paychecks. Those who pay the piper, as the saying goes, call the tune—not every note, but the overarching score—orchestration that may seem to be nowhere in particular because it is now almost everywhere, with an insistent drumbeat that after a while gets confused with the human heart. The political muzak keeps functioning as white noise, constant and familiar, with little variation, and loud enough to prevent us from hearing much of other sounds. To question the divine right of large corporations to occupy America's political throne is a lack of fealty that demands exclusion from the roundtables of mega-media discourse, where political "realities" are framed and re-framed every day.

For people on corporate payrolls, more than a little parental-company discretion is advised. Mainstream journalists are cases in point: Criticisms of government—and disparagements of the public sector overall—are far more acceptable than condemnations of corporate power. Yet the facts are cold and hard. "It is beyond doubt that the large corporation has always governed, most importantly by deciding whether untold numbers of people will live or die, will be injured, or will sicken," comments Morton Mintz, who left the *Washington Post* in 1988 after twenty-nine years as a reporter there; his attitude was rare in the newsroom. Media professionals are almost uniformly unwilling to voice anything that smacks of a systemic critique of the private-industry juggernaut.

III

One afternoon in late 1990, I appeared on a radio program with a national reporter for the *Los Angeles Times,* Bob Scheer, who'd been working for Southern California's dominant news outlet since the mid-1970s. On the air he acknowledged that "largely a lot of what we do is to be a conveyor belt of news from powerful government officials and so forth, they basically define what the news is." But Scheer framed his criticisms of the news industry to exclude the massive corporations with media companies among their many business holdings. "The issue is," he said, "is there pressure within any of these news organizations to gather news in a certain way? I don't think it comes from what they own."

In fact, much evidence to the contrary had long been available. Ben Bagdikian's classic book *The Media Monopoly,* first published in 1983 and later updated, provides a lot of specific examples showing that many news outlets—including the *L.A. Times*— skew what they publish and broadcast to serve the economic interests of owners. (Advertisers also have plenty of clout.) But to hear Scheer tell it, corporate power presented no problem: "As a working journalist—and I've been at the *L.A. Times* for fifteen years—I never felt any influence.... No one ever suggested that I go easy on anything that they happen to own.... I don't know that there's any connection between what the company owns and the way the news is reported."

The Times Mirror Company, parent corporation of the *Los Angeles Times*, is an economic powerhouse. As Bagdikian mentions in his book, the conglomerate "also owns other newspapers, cable systems, book publishing houses, agricultural land, urban real estate, commercial printing plants, and other nonjournalistic operations." But on the radio show, Scheer made a point of saying: "I don't even know what the parent company owns, and I've been there fifteen years."

A former editor of the left-wing *Ramparts* magazine during the Vietnam War, Bob Scheer went on to become one of the most independent-minded and enterprising reporters at the *Los Angeles Times*. That makes his expressed attitudes all the more significant—indicating the limits of acceptable analysis within mega-media journalism.

Let's take Scheer at his word: "I don't even know what the parent company owns, and I've been there fifteen years." Such an absence of curiosity is remarkable, especially for an investigative reporter. But in an odd way it dovetails neatly with the claim that media ownership doesn't really affect content. The most basic goal of owners—maximizing profits—usually eludes scrutiny, even though the pursuit of that goal restricts journalists every day. The boundaries may be invisible (though, we have reason to suspect, well understood), and all the more effective as constraints because they need not be imposed in any heavy-handed or "unprofessional" manner. In fact, the internalized constraints, with all their unspoken taboos, have come to seem integral to professionalism.

Corporate control is not interference in the newsroom—if you own an institution you aren't interfering in it, you're running it. Orwell anyone? *The conditioned reflex of "stopping short, as though by instinct, at the threshold of any dangerous thought." The doublethink process "has to be conscious, or it would not be carried out with sufficient precision, but it also has to be unconscious, or it would bring with it a feeling of falsity and hence of guilt."*

The debilitating obstacles that face journalists—and the rest of us—are primarily institutional. If we push hard to challenge the institutions around us, the struggle can change us for the better in the process. Rather than succumbing to the media manipulation that continues to foreclose better options, we can tune up our personal and collective "radar screens" to track unidentified flying propaganda. Determination to battle for more autonomy over our own possibilities—as individuals, as people communicating with each other, and as a society—opens up new and vital horizons.

In contrast, evading the truth of corporate power over news media is a disorienting mental traffic pattern that keeps tromping a path of political confusion. False mappings of society immobilize us to the great extent that we trust public mythologies more than firsthand realities. Imagine if Rand McNally and its competitors issued maps that had little resemblance to actual streets and highways and terrain. To the extent that we believed those maps, we'd be unable to go much of anywhere; we wouldn't be able to plan our journeys, or meet up with other people; for that matter we wouldn't even really know where we were.

"The news" and punditry provide orientation—guiding the public's perception and navigation of the world. At various times, on various subjects, the media compass needle may actually be pointing south, north, east or west; it's no accident that conventional accounts of politics are disorienting, since they take citizens on detours every day—away from clarity about power: who wields it, how, and why. (Astute investors would never make the mistake of trying to get their bearings from the "A" sections of daily newspapers.) As informative compasses, the mass media indicate much more about how those in power want us to perceive and navigate the world than about how the world really is.

Popularized renderings of reality, however phony, supply us with shared illusions, suitable for complying with authorized itineraries, the requisite trips through never-never lands of public pretense. Privately, we struggle to make sense of our experiences; perhaps we can create some personal space so that our own perceptions and emotions have room to stretch. But the limits of privatized solutions are severe. Public spheres determine the very air we breathe and the social environments of our lives. The standard detours meander through imposing landscapes. Beyond the outer limits of customary responses, uncharted territory is "weird"—certainly not familiar from watching TV or reading daily papers. Following in the usual footsteps seems to be safer.

Confusion about politics and power denies us clues as to where to go from here. Anne Wilson Schaef has identified pivotal results of such confusion:

> First, it keeps us powerless and controllable. No one is more controllable than a confused person; no society is more controllable than a confused society. Politicians know this better than anyone, and that is why they use innuendos, veiled references, and out-and-out lies instead of speaking clearly and truthfully.

> Second, it keeps us ignorant. Professionals give their clients confusing information cloaked in intimidating language that lay-people cannot understand. They preserve their "one-up" status while preventing us from learning about our own bodies, our legal rights, and our psychology.

> Third, it keeps us from taking responsibility for our own lives. No one expects confused people to own up to the things they think, say, or do, or face the truth about who they are.

> Fourth, it keeps us busy. When we must spend all our time and energy trying to figure out what is going on, we have none left over for reflecting on the system, challenging it, or exploring alternatives to it.

These have the combined effect of keeping us stuck within the system. And this, I believe, is the primary purpose of confusion. A confused person will stay within the system because the thought of moving out of it is too frightening. It takes a certain amount of clarity to try new things, walk new roads, and cross new bridges, and confusion makes clarity and risk taking impossible.

Mass media encourage us—viewers, listeners, readers—to suspend disbelief, willingly or otherwise. Stalked by propaganda wolves in chic clothing, we are the intended sheep. Conformity is disguised with appearances of diversity—just as silence about what matters most is in no way inconsistent with constant verbiage. "The great triumphs of propaganda have been accomplished, not by doing something, but by refraining from doing," Aldous Huxley observed. "Great is truth, but still greater, from a practical point of view, is silence about truth.... But silence is not enough. If persecution, liquidation and the other symptoms of social friction are to be avoided, the positive sides of propaganda must be made as effective as the negative. The most important Manhattan Projects of the future will be vast government-sponsored enquiries into what the politicians and the participating scientists will call 'the problem of happiness'—in other words, the problem of making people love their servitude."

Getting people to "love their servitude" is a tall order, but in America more modest conditioning has proved sufficient to make quiescence a common way of life. Within a pseudo-security state, the constant rush to desensitize has become a generic fix. To lives of quiet desperation, and to an ailing body politic, mass media are among the key institutions that administer anesthesia without surgery.

IV

"Public" TV and radio are supposed to be different—an alternative. Over the years, the "MacNeil/-Lehrer NewsHour," "All Things Considered" and "Morning Edition" have gained credibility and trust among millions of college-educated people, an audience heavily concentrated in professional circles (including many liberals and more than a few leftists), where restive responses could be especially troublesome to upper-echelon managers and policy elites.

When push comes to shove, for instance when the American Flag goes up and the troops go out, the news operations of PBS and NPR are among the country's most regimented; during the Gulf War in early 1991, they shamelessly served the war-makers (a role briefly reprised in summer 1993 when U.S. missiles struck an Iraqi office complex and a number of nearby civilians in Baghdad). The manipulation—usually a bit more subtle than at times of U.S. military attack—is a year-round reality, as the media watch group FAIR has documented with studies of the guest lists and sources of "MacNeil/Lehrer" and NPR's daily news programs. A narrow range—of voices, sound-bites, commentators and analysis—comes to seem normal, even exemplary. After all, the news is in-depth, with many sentences in a row; our intelligence does not seem to be insulted.

Bogus alternatives of the NPR/PBS variety are part of a mass media bandwagon pulling news consumers along on a short conceptual leash. The absence of critical imagination has been normalized. Big-name journalists, affecting sharp-eyed realism and attention to realpolitik, preen their credentials of discernment and independence. In news media, as in politics, only your essential passivity is sought. (All that advertisers and "underwriters" want are your purchases; all that politicians want are your votes.) It's called *programming.*

The puffed-up men and occasional women on network political shows are there to convey normalcy, providing the erudite ambience of in-control continuity from those who know best. They are On The Case. Anointed, seemingly confident, practiced and glib, functioning as if professional choruses in some upside down Greek play. They serve as inverted Cassandras: The real tragedy is that they are so widely believed.

Political battles are largely struggles over perception; how we see the world has everything to do with how we will live in it. Dominant assumptions— like familiar gases—are seldom noted, but they keep entering bloodstreams, flooding brains and hearts.

Mainstream media are busily focusing views away from possibilities that could undermine management. The mold of prevailing thought is not to be broken: "Real" politics is presented as the art of the possible, not a battleground for human imperatives. And, the bottom line ultimately being the bottom line, the system's loyalty is always to itself, never to any individual. So, at the top of government, Bill Clinton the man may outlive his usefulness, as Bush and Carter and Nixon did before him. The president is a CEO of sorts, and those who have made the "hiring" possible are certain to want acceptable returns on their investments.

Of course big business is always looking for new products to put on the market, and major presidential contenders are no exception. A quarter-century ago, when *The Selling of the President, 1968* came out, the book's cover featured a photo of Nixon on a cigarette pack—and the imagery caused an uproar; now we take it for granted that candidates will be sold like automobiles or deodorant. But the creation of politician-products runs parallel with broader inventions; a power elite that can heavily edit the past and distort the present also reserves the right to concoct scenarios for the future.

Television lights up homes everywhere with its narcotic glow; stupefication par excellence, now enhanced with numerous cable channels and, we are told, the advent of interactive TV technology. The pretense is that You Are There, or you have choices; the reality, much more likely, is that you aren't anywhere, and you can choose from the choices that have already been made for you. The delusion of "choice" from an array of televised (and corporately backed) programs is parallel to the delusion of choice from an array of pre-screened (and corporately backed) presidential candidates.

What shines through the screens makes a show of any and all matters, from the situation comedy to the latest war. Yet there is much self-congratulation and hype about how TV has brought war into our living rooms—a claim so ludicrous that one might think it's sometimes necessary to dig shrapnel out of the sofa after watching the news on television, as Mark Crispin Miller has commented: "What do we see when we sit at home and watch a war? Do we experience an actual event? In fact, that 'experience' is fundamentally absurd. Most obviously, there is the incongruity of scale, the radical disjunction of locations. While a war is among the biggest things that can ever happen to a nation or people, devastating families, blasting away the roofs and walls, we see it compressed and miniaturized on a sturdy little piece of furniture, which stands and shines at the very center of our household. And TV contains warfare in subtler ways. While it may confront us with the facts of death, bereavement, mutilation, it immediately cancels out the memory of that suffering, replacing its own pictures of despair with a commercial, upbeat and inexhaustibly bright."

In effect, "The TV newsman comforts us as John Wayne comforted our grandparents, by seeming to have the whole affair in hand.... Since no one seems to live on television, no one seems to die there. And the medium's temporal facility deprives all terminal moments of their weight."

Being numb to untoward events is in sync with being passive. For mass media, this is a perfect fit. Television, a powerful numb-er, asks that we do nothing—"don't touch that dial"—except go out and buy things. Everything is well-produced, including the latest war; especially one made in the USA.

The slaughter of approximately 200,000 Iraqis in a six-week period drew on the accumulated capital of America's numbing, as crucial to the Gulf War's success as the monetary resources of the United States, Saudi Arabia and Kuwait's rich families. Day after day, with talking heads galore and not a talking heart to be found on the networks, the anchors filled the media frames with their euphemistic jargon about "air strikes," "collateral damage" and "pounding enemy targets." Draining life from discussions of life-and-death subjects, what those who dominated the airwaves and print media kept conveying with their flat tones was that the wholesale destruction of human life could be discussed with pride; the effect was to fog up the horrors that the war entailed at every moment. Correspondents mouthed the language of the military, with human realities rarely even mentioned. Air Force officers, shown in pool video interviews, described the bombing runs in computer terms. "I just see blips on the screen," said one. And we saw the war's human devastation reported as blips on our TV screens.

Television powerfully normalizes duplicity; winks and nods become unnecessary. Advertising can have tremendous impact on people even if they "understand" cerebrally that the ads are untruthful and manipulative; the same goes for news reporting. Cognitive skepticism is a flimsy barrier when hard-driving media falsehoods constantly batter against it.

Anne Wilson Schaef describes television as one of the habitual commodities that "make us numb to our own reality—to seeing what we see and knowing what we know." But behind the madness of TV is an exceedingly lucrative method. Informing, entertaining and selling become interchangeable. Replete with technical virtuosity, ads on television have become "art forms"; small wonder that Star Wars movie-maker Lucas Films got into producing TV commercials in a big way. Sales pitches should be entertaining, and entertainment should be pitching for consumption. And when people are reticent to share unscreened aspects of who they are and how they feel, life is stunting itself—imitating the constraints of the tube, absorbing television's complementary messages that keep hectoring for supine quietude among the population.

The anesthetic effect renders us comfortably

numb yet uncomfortably on edge, swaddled in media insulation. The passivity of the TV experience is good training for watching history go by. History—even when it's in the process of occurring—comes across as some kind of gaseous time in a shattered bottle. A long dead letter. Here in the USA, the announced "end of history" is more akin to the end of open feeling and the substitution of the facade for the authentic in public matters. Immersed in such a synthetic meta-world, "history" can only be disconnected from the moment—eviscerated, both privatized and falsified, part mystery and part dusty facts, like a phone book filled with information and drained of truth.

V

For several decades we've been undergoing the refinement of multimedia inculcation—evermore overbearing and veiled—like pollution that becomes less obvious the more it is added to what is already widespread. Yet many of the purveyed hypocrisies are hardly subtle.

Orwell wrote in *1984* about a process that "in short, means protective stupidity." The approach involves "holding two contradictory beliefs in one's mind simultaneously, and accepting both of them." Today, for politicians and their aides, Orwellian maneuvers become second nature: "To tell deliberate lies while genuinely believing in them, to forget any fact that has become inconvenient, and then, when it becomes necessary again, to draw it back from oblivion for just so long as it is needed, to deny the existence of objective reality and all the while to take account of the reality which one denies—all this is indispensably necessary."

Basic hypocrisy is apt to seem obscure when grim ironies go unremarked and glaring contradictions are not illuminated by mass media. Big-budget PR operations function with the assumption that people can't think of everything; their thoughts have to be guided in certain directions and away from others. "We know that crimes against humanity have occurred, and we know when and where they occurred," U.S. Secretary of State Lawrence Eagleburger declared in a December 1992 speech. "We know, moreover, which forces committed those crimes and under whose command they operated. And we know, finally, who the political leaders are to whom these military commanders were—and still are—responsible."

The brazenness of doublethink is enough to take your breath away; in fact, it takes away many people's breath, quite literally. The secretary of state was speaking about political leaders and military commanders of Serbia. But it was, as well, a perfect description of Eagleburger and those he had worked closely with during the Gulf War a couple of years earlier. That Eagleburger was in a Republican administration is beside the point; if doublethink is anything, it is bipartisan. As he campaigned for the 1992 Democratic presidential nomination, Bill Clinton repeatedly spoke of the necessity that the United States "be leading the Desert Storms in the 21st century." Five months into his presidency, Clinton ordered a missile attack on Iraq and then backed it up with rhetoric from the same lexicon used by President Bush.

Mass media, predisposed to impute the noblest

of motives to presidents when the U.S. military swings into lethal action, puffed up Clinton after he gave the order to launch two-dozen missiles that hit an Iraqi intelligence building and residential homes in Baghdad. *Time* Magazine dubbed Clinton's televised announcement from the Oval Office "one of his finest moments; he struck the right tone, reasoned but forceful." The next day, the *New York Times* reported, "a near-defiant sense of pride was tangible at the White House." The *Times* went on: "While it was clearly not a motivation for the strike, the likelihood that Mr. Clinton's standing in public-opinion polls would rise, as support for most presidents has after military actions, appeared to have contributed to the buoyant mood."

To the standard buzzwords and catch-phrases of American newspeak, television reports add a narcissistic patina, a translucent glaze over "reality," repeating particular words and carefully selected visuals with logarithmic intensity. The repetition is key. Exceptional articles and broadcasts do run counter to the norm once in a while, but the essence of propaganda is repetition—the daily dollops of news and views dominating the nation, steering most people away from unapproved avenues of thinking. The "skipthought" process is so widespread that it melts into the air, everywhere and unremarkable, like an odor so constant that it seems to have no smell.

Impressions of politicians, seen through media lenses, often amount to not much more than assessments of production values. It's largely on that basis that some people "like" Clinton despite his betrayal of many principles important to them. Media appearances are inevitably deceiving; they invite us to react with a passive sense of aesthetics. From corporate boardrooms to Capitol Hill cloakrooms, from the Executive Mansion to the Pentagon, our torpor is much sought after, and appreciated. More than our favor, it is our prior restraint that is curried.

Huge fortunes keep being made on the prudent bet that we will remain anesthetized. The more that human imagination can be curtailed, the more it can be profitably sublimated and channeled. There is no devious master plot—only the steady workings of a system masterfully encouraging acceptance, while transforming concepts of what has to be and what cannot be.

Preoccupied with revved-up mass media offerings, we're on treadmills of variegated conformity. Only authentic imagination can lead us elsewhere. But it is not imagination to picture ourselves as characters in a popular TV adventure show, or to identify with one side in a "debate" on the "MacNeil/Lehrer NewsHour," or to prefer one of the budget versions in a House-Senate conference committee; when we select from the options already handed down from on high, we can only imagine what has already been imagined for us. When thought processes are corralled by received notions of realism, then possibilities for independent actions are fenced off.

In contrast, as cultural critic Joyce Nelson says, *imagination* "is a truly revolutionary force, allowing us to conceive of alternatives. It is 'radical' in the deepest sense of that word: transforming things at their root, opening up new possibilities, challenging and suspending (for the moment, or longer) the status quo." What we are able to think prefigures what we might be able to do.

"Political thought, no less than any other kind, takes place in imagination," Rose Goldsen wrote. "In imagination we move around the social system so that we can peer at social reality first from this vantage point, then from that one, each time taking our bearings from the different slant.... Social meanings emerge as we imagine the situation as it could otherwise have been (or be). The otherwise...can exist only in imagination."

Today, looking out at the USA's gritty and perfumed landscape, we may feel that we're growing old in a bleak civilization, an era mundane and terrible. The fact that wonderful people are capable of magnificent creations makes our socialized dead-ends all the more difficult to bear, and all the more urgent to confront.

Precious threads of human continuity and vibrant culture persist. But in contrast to George Orwell's nightmare, there is no need for complete uniformity here; domination will suffice, as social machinery mass-produces and homogenizes human awareness to an immense and accelerating degree. The ability to numb and delude is the ability to control. And the propaganda of anesthesia seems to be nearly everywhere; the hollowing out of words is an enterprise parallel with the hollowing out of lives.

A haze surrounds us; mass-media fog banks sweep in front of vision, clouding imagination, allowing only glimpses of better possibilities. Under conditions of low visibility, the present moves like the horizon along a centrist road: attentive to the synthetic mist, and missing the outlines of humanity unseen.

Six

The White House of "the Middle Class"

In the glow of Bill Clinton's election, some readers of the *Progressive* had been annoyed when they picked up the magazine's December 1992 issue. An editorial reviewed the Clinton campaign—"he acted as if there were no homeless and no poor people in this country, so much did he bray about 'the middle class'"—and then made a prophetic prediction: "Since he knows he'll be hit from the right, it is to his right that he will move. And since he, his advisers, and the pundits are interpreting his victory as a vindication of his rightward strategy, there's no reason to expect he'll abandon it." Sure enough.

All the facile talk about "the middle class" has become a sleight-of-tongue way to evade the huge gaps between economic strata of our society. The frame of reference keeps moving in advantageous directions to aid class warfare from the top down. Reporting from Southern California in the summer of 1993, under the headline "G.O.P. Blitz Against Budget Puts Democrats on Defensive," the *New York Times* explained on its front page that Clinton was not offering much to "people earning more than $115,000, which is middle class in this high-cost region." Six figures a year, and part of the beleaguered middle class.

In 1993 the Clinton administration quickly dropped all but the thinnest pretenses of advocating for people with small incomes. Job programs were not worth fighting for. Aid to the cities wasn't even worth proposing...now that the election was over. Sparse resources would be sought for the projects touted as adding up to a new approach to social problems. It was neglect, scarcely more benign than usual. Nowhere to be found was any kind of White House proposal that might make a significant difference for large numbers of poor people. Urgency? Forget it. That precious commodity had to be reserved for political calculations.

Many of the poor are working very hard to eke out a living. But with only one out of seven people unionized in the U.S. workforce (compared with one out of three a few decades ago), the position of organized labor is weak. Bill Clinton seems to like it that way. His lackadaisical attitude toward raising the minimum wage reflects a general disinterest in doing much for workers, who see their real incomes and job security continuing to slip. When the Bank of America reported gigantic profits in 1993 while reducing the hours of employees to deprive them of benefits, that was part of a nationwide trend; the Clinton presidency abets such "efficiency" measures.

Some minor reforms may include improvements at the National Labor Relations Board, flagrantly anti-union during the Reagan-Bush years. But Clinton—who got to the White House with strong union support—is no friend of labor, as his key appointees indicate. "The jury is still out on whether the traditional union is necessary for the new work-place," Labor Secretary Robert Reich stated six months into Clinton's term. Commerce Secretary Ron Brown chimed in: "Unions are O.K. where they are. And where they are not, it is not clear yet what sort of organization should represent workers." When the new Democratic administration named the chair of the presidential "Commission on the Future of Worker/Management Relations," the post went to John Dunlop—who was labor secretary in the Ford administration.

In the past, mainstream pundits have lam-pooned liberals as political cannibals too willing to devour their own. However, the much stronger ten-dency is to swallow concerns and go along to get along, especially with a Democrat in the Oval Office. Surely, by summer 1993, millions of Clinton voters were fuming about the new president's repeated def-erence to anti-progressive pressures. But—particu-larly among whites who considered themselves to be liberal—there was a lot of hesitation to criticize Clinton very loudly in public.

II

Yet some elected leaders did not hesitate. Many members of the Congressional Black Caucus set a good example, responding quickly and vehemently in early June 1993 when President Clinton with-drew his nomination of Lani Guinier to be assistant attorney general for civil rights. But when Clinton was asked at a mid-June news conference about the anger inside the Black Caucus, he claimed to have a good relationship with the group—and added that anyone who knew his record could not doubt his dedication to civil rights. A month later, at the annual conference of the N.A.A.C.P., the organization's chair William F. Gibson said that Clinton "kicked us in the teeth" by dropping Guinier. Such candor was badly needed; the taste of President Clinton's shoes was already familiar.

An articulate African-American law professor, Guinier had voiced alarm that some redistricting strategies "transformed the original goals of broad-based voter participation, reform, and authentic representation into the shorthand of counting elected black officials." In local elections, she suggested, innovative at-large voting systems could give each citizen the right to cast several votes—perhaps one vote for each of a number of candidates, or all votes for one candidate. "Guinier advocates a profoundly democratic solution to the perpetual racism and corruption of local electoral districting," wrote a contributing editor of the *Nation,* Bruce Shapiro. "It could help end the apartheid that still permeates U.S. electoral politics. Her approach could also crack monolithic local political machines and open up electoral politics to a range of ideas and political interests formerly locked out of the system."

When Clinton abandoned his nominee, the policy director of the People for the American Way Action Fund, Leslie Harris, told the press: "This cave-in is a betrayal not just of Lani Guinier but of basic fairness." Yet Clinton's actions seemed less bothersome to many other white-led liberal organizations, inclined to see pragmatism in the president's behavior. Sometimes the contention was that, in his heart of hearts, Clinton was truly well-intentioned—he just had to deal with the tough dilemmas of politics in high places.

Guinier's refusal to walk the plank made presidential aides angry at her—"for failing to be a team player," as *Time* put it. The magazine quoted an administration official, unnamed and resentful: "Lani was not going to pull herself out. It's the M.O. of the civil-rights movement that they are not satisfied until they can go out, declare defeat and say, 'We got screwed.' That's what they wanted. That's what they got." The quote spoke volumes about attitudes at the Clinton White House. It also echoed past liberal responses to civil-rights activists unwilling to compromise with a benevolent Democratic president.

Twenty-nine years earlier, at the 1964 Democratic National Convention in Atlantic City, the president's operatives were infuriated by the refusal of the Mississippi Freedom Democratic Party to go along with the Johnson administration's "compromise"—a couple of at-large seats for the MFDP while the state's all-white delegation could remain in place. The Mississippi Freedom Democratic Party's sixty-eight delegates represented 63,000 black people who'd signed up with the MFDP, in a state where authorities barred blacks from registering to vote; police and other bigots had inflicted extreme violence on many voting-rights workers.

"We didn't come all this way for no two seats when all of us is tired," Fannie Lou Hamer explained in Atlantic City. But Hubert Humphrey's young protégé Walter Mondale emerged from deliberations to tell the press: "It may not satisfy everybody, the extremes on the right nor the extremes on the left, but we think it is a just compromise. We think it is based soundly on the law, we think it clearly recognizes without compromising the basic devotion of this party to human rights, and we think it represents and sets the stage for the overwhelming victory of the man who more than anybody else in the world represents the cause of justice and law today, President Lyndon Baines Johnson." As author Nicolaus Mills recounts, "In liberal circles the MFDP's rejection of the White House offer was proof that the [Freedom] party did not know how the game of politics was played."

Sophisticated counsel about how to play political games, coming from self-declared pragmatists, was as widespread then as three decades later. Anthony Lewis, writing in the *New York Times* of August 27, 1964, maintained that Mississippi insurgents like Fannie Lou Hamer didn't understand all the progress they'd already made: "It is plainly difficult for those long deprived of the most elementary rights to move from the first actions of demonstrations to the necessarily slowed and often more frustrating business of exerting influence by means of the vote and other political action," Lewis lamented. Unhappy about intransigence within the freedom movement, he worried about trouble ahead: "The liberal concern is that a failure of the civil rights movement to accept the ambiguities and frustrations of politics—a decision to go on demonstrating instead—could have dangerous consequences in the long run." Media-lauded black "moderates," notably Bayard Rustin and Roy Wilkins, were outspoken in their disapproval of the MFDP's failure to compromise.

"We learned the hard way that even though we

had all the law and all the righteousness on our side—that white man is not going to give up his power to us," Fannie Lou Hamer said later. "We have to build our own power. We have to win every single political office we can, where we have a majority of black people." She added: "The question for black people is not, when is the white man going to give us our rights, or when is he going to give us good education for our children, or when is he going to give us jobs—if the white man gives you any-thing—just remember when he gets ready he will take it right back. We have to take for ourselves."

The choices faced by the Mississippi Freedom Democratic Party reverberate today. An organizer for the MFDP, Charles Sherrod of the Student Nonviolent Coordinating Committee, put it this way:

> We were asserting a moral declaration to this country that the political mind must be con-cerned with much more than the expedient; that there are real issues in this country's politics and "race" is one.... We could have accepted the compromise, called it a victory and gone back to Mississippi, carried on the shoulders of millions of Negroes across the country as their champi-ons. But we love the ideals of our country; they mean more than a moment of victory. We are what we are—hungry, beaten, unvictorious, job-less, homeless, but thankful to have the strength to fight. This is honesty, and we refuse to com-promise here. It would have been a lie to accept that particular compromise. It would have said to blacks across the nation and the world that we share the power, and that is a lie! The "liber-als" would have felt great relief for a job well done. The Democrats would have laughed again

at the segregationist Republicans and smiled that their own "Negroes" were satisfied. That is a lie! We are a country of racists with a racist heritage, a racist economy, a racist language, a racist religion, a racist philosophy of living, and we need a naked confrontation with ourselves.

Bill Clinton has been careful to bypass any such "naked confrontation with ourselves." And mass media usually seem appreciative.

An exception to the dominant media spin on Clinton's handling of the Lani Guinier nomination appeared as an "Editorial Notebook" post-mortem in the *New York Times.* Written by Brent Staples, the piece provided sharp analysis of the Clinton-style race card: "The Guinier debacle was damaging in the racial sense, partly because Mr. Clinton's record on race is so problematic. Yes, there are black faces in the cabinet. But racial gambits played by the Clinton campaign still hang heavy in the air. As a candidate, Mr. Clinton seemed obsessed with proving that he could be stern with black folks. To show toughness on crime, he executed Rickey Ray Rector, a brain-damaged black man who seemed unaware that death was permanent. To neutralize the black left, Mr. Clinton scolded Jesse Jackson from Mr. Jackson's own podium at the Rainbow Coalition in Washington. This angered even Mr. Jackson's detractors, who saw it for the spanking-the-blacks routine that it was. During the Los Angeles riots, Mr. Clinton managed so feeble a response that he sounded like George Bush. As a candidate, Mr. Clinton condemned Mr. Bush's policy of forcing boatloads of refugees back to Haiti, and praised the court that found that approach illegal. As president,

The White House of "the Middle Class"

Mr. Clinton embraced the policy he'd criticized. Against this backdrop, black Democrats could well see the sacrificing of Ms. Guinier as one more back of the hand from Bill."

III

The reality is that we cannot know what is in a president's heart. To guess is often an exercise in projection, and always a waste of time. It's impossible to know what President Clinton "really" feels or believes. But even if, for the sake of discussion, we assume his best intentions as a person, the excuses commonly made for him are political cul-de-sacs:

Denouncing Clinton will only help the Republicans. The same was said to justify subservience to previous Democratic presidents: as Truman handed down his loyalty orders and paved the way for the witchhunts; as Kennedy waffled on civil rights and promoted counterinsurgency wars in the Third World; as Johnson jettisoned the war on poverty in favor of the war on Vietnam; as Carter expanded military spending at the expense of domestic social programs, and continued backing for brutal regimes in places like El Salvador, Iran and the Philippines.

Clinton can't be expected to fight for what he can't win. With much media prompting, we're apt to miss the key point: Clinton can't win what he refuses to fight for. And *we* can't win what *we* don't fight for.

We have to be realistic. What does that mean? The finest moments of political leadership and activism—and the most wondrous turning points of history—have come with refusals to accept the reigning definitions of "realism."

Congress won't let Clinton do what he'd like to do. If a cause were important enough to Clinton, he would make himself part of a national effort to get behind it. In the absence of such activities by Clinton on issues that matter most, he is part of the same obstacle that Congress is.

Whether Clinton means well or means ill, whether he is sincere or a snake, the path should be the same for us—push for what we believe in, and declare political war on his unacceptable policies and priorities. President Clinton's inner state is a conjectural matter, but his outward behavior is not. A leader of the Log Cabin Republicans (a gay-rights group that had refused to endorse Bush in '92) put it well after six months of Clinton's presidency: "It's clear to the religious right now that if you hit him hard enough, he'll roll." The left never hit him hard enough.

The fact that Clinton is under frequent attack from the right is liable to dissuade leftists from denouncing him. But the successes of those right-wing attacks attest to just how much the left has failed to exert counterpressure. The news media's admonitions that Clinton must be "centrist" and not "liberal" have served as warning shots across the presidential bow. In the absence of much fire from the opposite perspective, Clinton opts to tack further away from progressive directions.

For each of us, rationales are always available for keeping quiet about truth. The silence can be dressed in the stylish clothing of prudence and wisdom; decisions to wink at what is wrong can be elevated to the status of pragmatic sophistication.

There is always a reason to shut up, or to mute a voice that could be forthright, turning it into a private lament or public mumble. There is always the appearance of unity to maintain, another election to finesse ('96), a greater evil to defeat (Republicans), a hundred and one inducements for going with the program. But dissembling and avoidance tend to be habit-forming. Lies, told if only by remaining silent, can come to seem quite proper; sad and enraging truths come to seem unnecessary to utter—intemperate, exaggerated, ill-advised.

White House actions and inaction that would have drawn cries of outrage during the Reagan and Bush eras can often slide by with meager opposition now—no matter how much suffering results. The rationales are plentiful. (*"Republicans are a lot worse... Unless we support Clinton, he won't get re-elected... We need to be patient..."*) The prevailing ultra-pragmatism throws cold water on fiery grassroots activism that can expose power and confront its consequences. Media mists, and the smoke-and-mirrors of Democratic rhetoric, fog the grimness of the status quo.

IV

Amid all the talk of "change," routine economic brutality is undisturbed: across the United States, whether in South Central or the South Bronx or the hills of West Virginia, and overseas in countless communities of misery. Meanwhile, in bank towers from Manhattan to Bonn to Tokyo, and in suites of the benign-sounding International Monetary Fund, financiers make a killing each day—corporate wizards operating behind Oz-like curtains, re-enforcing opulence and untold anguish. While multitudes of children and adults remain crushed against walls of structural cruelty, the president and Congress maintain the tradition of tacitly abetting their torment; there is not even a rhetorical war on poverty, only purposeful surrender to "market forces."

All the while, left-leaning minds are encouraged to wander toward pleasant thoughts, perhaps to rejoice in low-budget social projects or the spittle-and-polish of a humanistic White House facade. We must "help Clinton to succeed," or at least not add to his burden. The big sirens of politics beckon us each to avert our eyes from ugly truths; preoccupied with what Clinton might do, we remain welcome to privatize our anger, and to hope.

The extent of such quiescence has been a delight for strategists bent on pushing the country's perceived "center" rightward. Saluted as above ideology, Clinton's much-vaunted centrism is an ideological flag: cemented to corporate terra firma and festooned with ribbons of "change." Pleased with the presence of a Democrat atop the Executive Branch after all these years, we may be eager to avoid seeming marginal; yet we assure our marginality by being pacified with little more than symbols. When we grasp at tokens and find solace in soothing presidential rhetoric, powers-that-be love to play us for chumps.

Consider these sentences from the *San Francisco Chronicle* about President Clinton's health care plan: "Former Clinton campaign adviser Bruce Fried believes that, in the long run, the president can afford to displease his critics on the left. 'My sense is that they will fall in line,' he said. 'Where else do they go?'"

The White House of "the Middle Class"

The same question was asked in the mid-1960s. Thousands of activists answered it with creative energies that built a movement for peace and social justice. One of those activists, Martin Luther King Jr., said in a speech to the California Democratic Council three weeks before his death: "On some positions, cowardice asks the question: 'Is it safe?' Expediency asks the question: 'Is it politic?' Vanity asks the question: 'Is it popular?' But conscience asks the question: 'Is it right?'"

The "moderation" of the convention that nominated Clinton is now perpetuating the devastation of uncounted lives. "The Democratic Party's platform isn't going to do anything to bring homelessness to an end," said Charles King, director of the nonprofit Housing Works organization in New York City, interviewed a few blocks from the festivities at Madison Square Garden. "If we want to discard whole segments of the population, we might have that choice. But we have to be honest about what we are doing. More than that, I think it's important to know that we are creating for ourselves a problem that will become intractable. The AIDS epidemic has been fueled by homelessness, as has the TB epidemic. I think the important point to be made—whether it's homelessness or AIDS or other systemic problems that we're faced with—is that these problems aren't intractable. It's not that we don't have the money. It's not that we don't have the resources. It's simply that we don't have the political will to stand up and say: *These are the costs. These are the things we need to do.*"

While the White House is less mean-spirited under Clinton than it was under Bush, the continuity between administrations is profound. A homeless person would have trouble seeing a difference. So would someone with AIDS. So would a Haitian who tried to escape a homeland of terror in 1993, only to be scooped up from a boat in mid-ocean and sent back by the United States government. Or one of the world's millions of children with pencil-thin limbs and bloated belly. Or a torture victim in any number of countries where aid money for the entrenched regime keeps pouring in from the U.S. government...

All too often, the Clinton paradigm gets ugly. Take immigrant-bashing, for instance. "In an effort to be seen as 'leading' on the issue of immigration," the Committee for Health Rights in Central America reported in an August 1993 bulletin, "President Clinton has put forward proposals to restrict access to the right to asylum for refugees.... Clinton's plan denies refugees access to judicial review and due process by leaving the initial screening up to individual INS agents without providing access to a translator or even an attorney. One New York immigrant rights leader concluded that 'Clinton's plan gives less right of due process to refugees than to someone who receives a parking ticket.'"

Publicized as one of the most far-left Democrats to enter the U.S. Senate in 1993, Barbara Boxer of California soon jumped on the xenophobic bandwagon. Only a few months into a six-year seat, Senator Boxer was scapegoating immigrants—blaming them for hard times and proposing heavy U.S. military patrols along the Mexican border. The Committee for Health Rights didn't mince words: Boxer and the state's other Democratic senator, Dianne Feinstein, "are asserting that California's economic woes are due to our large immigrant population. Despite the support they garnered from progressive voters, both have made proposals which previously were only advocated by the most right wing of California's politicians."

Since Bill Clinton became president, we haven't lacked for the symbols of caring at the top of the federal government. But would you want your life to depend on the Clinton administration's courage in standing for principle?

Clinton managed to nominate his entire cabinet well before his inauguration, but did not name a White House AIDS coordinator until June 25, 1993. Apologists used as an excuse the prior rejection of the job by others. But Clinton placed AIDS at such a low priority that he crippled the post from the outset. The *New York Times* mentioned in early summer that "as the months went on, the appointment was repeatedly delayed as several people turned down the job, amid doubts that the appointee would have real power or access to the president to overcome the expected political pitfalls."

Showy symbolism and compassion worn on televised sleeves—such as Clinton giving a thumbs-up to Michael Jackson's touching speech about children with AIDS at Inaugural festivities—went a long way to insulate Clinton from criticism as he kept AIDS concerns low on his agenda. After waiting five months as president, Clinton made a tepid selection for "AIDS czar"—Kristine Gebbie, repeatedly described by colleagues who served with her on the Reagan administration's Commission on AIDS as a "consensus builder." No firebrand or galvanizer for AIDS czar—and no passionate advocate of fighting AIDS in the presidential "bully pulpit"—as the AIDS catastrophe continues to claim our loved ones.

Often cited is the real difference that Clinton-ism makes for abortion rights. But definitions of "choice" tend to be quite narrow, as the White House showed in 1993 when it refused to take a position for poor women's access to abortion. That refusal was foreshadowed by the '92 campaign. The bigger picture got lost.

"What is needed is to look at 'choice' in the broad-er framework," pediatrician Helen Rodriguez-Trias, pointed out in the midst of hoopla over Clinton and Gore as pro-choice candidates. Rodriguez-Trias, then president-elect of the American Public Health Association, urged attention to current realities:

> Today in the U.S. most of the poor people are women and children. About one in five children in the United States lives in a household below the poverty line that is not even generous to begin with. So we're talking about real dire poverty for millions of women and children in this country. So the issue is: what are the choic-es? How do we define "choices"? Do we define "choice" as the right to have or not to have a child, to have a child and have that child grow up in a home that has access to food, to cloth-ing, to education, to health care?.... The notion of partial reproductive rights by looking just at whether you have the right to choose or not to choose abortion—that's necessary, because that's a line of struggle, but that's definitely not enough and does not define the needs of mil-lions of American women and children.

President Clinton's ostensible strong points—such as the Supreme Court—are not as strong as they might seem. When Clinton put Ruth Bader Ginsburg on the highest court, she was not likely to be a heavy counterweight. Ginsburg's thirteen-year record on the federal appeals court bench shows her frequently lining up with conservative judges; a study of her 1987 cases revealed that in divided decisions, she voted with the right-wing judge Robert Bork a total of 85 percent of the time—more than twice as often as with the liberal jurist Patricia Wald.

Bill Clinton seems to reflexively skate across the veneer of single-issue politics, making appointments that are surface symbols. With women's groups demanding female cabinet members, Clinton responded with his first pick for attorney general— ace corporate legal-whiz Zoë Baird, the chief counsel for Aetna Life and Casualty, who previously ran General Electric's legal department. Black individuals sounding much more like Malcolm Forbes than Malcolm X in the Clinton cabinet—Ron Brown, Hazel O'Leary, Mike Espy—could be passed off as evidence of presidential commitment to black people.

In the light of subsequent events, the way that Clinton brought African-Americans into the upper reaches of his administration was telling; they did not represent blacks to the white power structure, but vice versa. "Although whites who bring blacks into formerly all-white workplaces talk a lot about integration, they seem at bottom to want the *appearance* of change without its substance," Roger Wilkins has observed. "The blacks who are deemed qualified for 'white' jobs are usually the most white-like in the population. The expectation—often

129

unconscious, I am sure—is that though the color in the class picture will look different, nothing in fact will have been changed. That may work where people are installing telephone lines or figuring out how to sell shock absorbers. But when it comes to making, shaping or analyzing public policy, that white hope is either fools' gold or a black's nightmare." Wilkins wrote those words more than a decade ago. And so in the Clinton era it often seems, yet again, that the more things "change," the more...

V

In dozens of countries around the world, regimes engaging in violent repression can apparently count on continued U.S. government largess, despite State Department noises of misgivings. An example: At the same time that Secretary of State Warren Christopher made a public statement about the need to improve the human rights situation in Turkey, the Clinton administration announced it was bestowing $336 million worth of military hardware on Turkey's government.

"Yet Turkey's human rights picture has become worse in the last year and a half," said Lois Whitman, deputy director of Helsinki Watch, in summer 1993. "In our recent missions to Turkey, we have found routine police torture of both political and common criminal suspects during interrogation. Moreover, Turkish security forces continue to shoot and kill peaceful demonstrators and to shoot and kill suspects in house raids, rather than arresting and trying them. In southeast Turkey more than 500 people were assassinated last year. The Turkish government has utterly failed to investigate these deaths and prosecute those responsible. Fifteen journalists have been assassinated since February 1992. Journals and newspapers are confiscated and banned. Reporters are beaten, detained and tortured, and journalists continue to be tried and sentenced for such offenses as 'insulting' Ataturk or the military, or 'disseminating separatist propaganda.' Kurds in southeast Turkey are detained and tortured, and forced either to act as 'village guards' for the security forces or to leave their homes and lands. Denied their cultural identity, Kurds continue to be sentenced for singing Kurdish songs. It is a crime to speak Kurdish at a trial or in another official setting."

Turkey, after all, is a solid U.S. military ally, having reaffirmed its value by joining in the Gulf War against Iraq in 1991. After five months in the White House, Clinton underscored his unity with the mentality of that warfare by ordering a U.S. missile attack on an intelligence complex in Baghdad; an administration spokesperson at the Pentagon said that a few of the cruise missiles had, regrettably, caused "collateral damage"—newspeak for *dead civilians* away from the target.

The main reason given for that attack was an unsubstantiated "plot," blamed on the Iraqi government, to assassinate George Bush during an early 1993 visit to Kuwait. (Imagine how many countries could, with similar reasoning, fire missiles at the CIA headquarters in Langley, Virginia, as retribution for the U.S. government's involvement in plots to assassinate political leaders in those countries.) Clinton was consistent in his support for the U.S. prerogative of bombing Iraq at will. He surprised

131

some observers in spring 1993, however, when he asked Congress to increase spending for the Central Intelligence Agency—after campaigning with a promise to cut the CIA budget by $7 billion during his first term.

How much the Clinton team would be willing to engage in direct military intervention remained to be seen. But it was no slouch at winking at vicious bombardment by allies, such as Israel's airborne siege of Lebanon in late July 1993—seven days that, in the phrases of the *New York Times,* "turned many southern Lebanese villages into ghost towns" and "displaced some 300,000 people"; more than 130 people (three Israelis among them) were reported dead, "and some 500 people, many of them Lebanese civilians, wounded." After several days of green-lighting the assaults with faint murmurs of disquiet, the U.S. State Department was pleased to get credit for brokering a cease-fire.

Continuity between the Bush and Clinton administrations was smooth. Clinton chose Martin Indyk as the National Security Council's "senior director for Near East and South Asian Affairs." His qualifications for the job included running the Washington Institute for Near East Policy, a group closely tied to the pro-Israel lobby. Indyk was the only Mideast analyst quoted in the *New York Times* edition that wrapped up news coverage of the October 1991 Arab-Israeli peace conference in Madrid; he profusely praised the Middle East diplomacy of Secretary of State James Baker.

Joining Indyk in the new president's inner circle on the region was Dennis B. Ross, appointed by Clinton in summer 1993 to serve as "special coordinator for the Middle East Peace Process." Ross was George Bush's main foreign policy adviser during the 1988 presidential campaign, and worked in his 1992 re-election effort. In the interim, at the State Department, Ross was a key assistant to James Baker—who offered high praise when Ross became a central player in the Democratic administration's policy-making: "There's nobody better on the problems and the intricacies and the history of the peace process."

Seamless bipartisan continuity was also apparent in White House relations with Russia. During 1993, Moscow's plunge into privatization inflicted terrible new hardships on most Russians, while delighting the International Monetary Fund, corporations in the West—and President Clinton, who boosted Boris Yeltsin at every opportunity. When the Russian president dissolved parliament on the first day of autumn, Clinton rushed to express enthusiasm for Yeltsin's blatantly unconstitutional move. Secretary of State Warren Christopher quickly defended the power grab, borrowing from Orwell to applaud "President Yeltsin and his program of democratic reform." Unequivocal backing from the U.S. government helped set the stage for early October's bloody clashes in Moscow. And, with the Russian parliament building charred from the military assault ordered by Yeltsin, the Clinton administration maintained its full support for a Russian autocrat ruling by decree.

By all accounts, Clinton came very close to ordering the resumption of nuclear testing in summer 1993, a move that would have shattered a *de facto* worldwide moratorium. (If he could, Clinton would probably have ordered half a nuclear test—to spiff up his credentials as a moderate.) His decision to foreclose U.S. tests for a year was no commitment to a comprehensive test ban; in fact, on October 5, 1993, Clinton responded to news of a Chinese nuclear test by announcing that he had "directed the Department of Energy to take such actions as are needed to put the U.S. in a position to be able to conduct nuclear tests next year." Nevertheless, the evident pressure not to resume testing was a testament to the value of grassroots organizing that for many years endeavored to halt atomic tests. Rather than ease up after Clinton's inauguration, many activists worked hard to generate what one of Clinton's top aides called "a firestorm of public opinion." Without that "firestorm," U.S. nuclear testing would have restarted in mid-1993.

But the nuclear-arms psychosis is alive and well. Under Clinton the government is going ahead with multibillion-dollar outlays for retooling the nuclear weapons assembly line. "The nuclear threat is still very much with us today," the California-based Peninsula Peace and Justice Center pointed out on Hiroshima Day 1993. "Right now, Pentagon planners are designing a whole new generation of nuclear weapons, with the approval and support of the Clinton administration. So-called micro-nukes, mini-nukes and tiny-nukes are being designed for use against the Third World. They are weapons designed to fight wars rather than deter them. President Clinton's budget includes $1.3 billion for the development of new nuclear weapons."

Plunging ahead with nuclear weaponry production, and accepting the 110 commercial nuclear power reactors on-line in the United States, Clinton has a stance toward radiation that is indicative of where his administration has headed on environmental issues generally. Mild modifications do not break the momentum of the daily large-scale assaults on nature that have been poisoning so much of the world around us.

The controversy over a Waste Technologies Industries plant in Ohio was supposed to showcase a sharp contrast between Bush-Quayle and Clinton-Gore. During the '92 campaign, Clinton vowed to prevent the W.T.I. toxic waste incinerator from opening. So did Al Gore—who spared no passion in denouncing W.T.I., a mammoth facility set to operate just 300 yards from an elementary school in the city of East Liverpool. Widely celebrated as the national green candidate, Gore used the W.T.I. issue to appeal for environmental votes. But two months after he became vice president, Gore was no longer talking about the need to block W.T.I.; instead, he spoke of federal obligations to its investors. In mid-March 1993, the Clinton administration's Environmental Protection Agency announced that it would not take action to bar the opening of W.T.I.

"So far the Clinton way of doing business is no different from the Bush way," investigative journalist Liane Clorfene-Casten wrote in September 1993. The implications for public health were foreboding. In a test burn, W.T.I. emitted large quantities of dioxin and mercury. "More than 300 chemicals have been approved for incineration there," she reported, "and once operations begin in earnest the stacks will be allowed to release 4.5 tons of lead, 1.5 tons of mercury, 100 tons of sulfur dioxide and

400 other highly toxic chemical substances each year.... Any release from the site, whether as a result of accident, explosion or misconduct, will likely wind up in the river—a source of drinking water for millions living in towns down-river." After Clinton and Gore made so much noise opposing the W.T.I. incinerator in 1992, why their turnaround after the election?

Clorfene-Casten provided some clues in a *Nation* magazine article:

> The incinerator project was begun under the aegis of financier Jackson Stephens, chairman of Stephens Inc., one of the nation's largest investment banking companies, based in Little Rock, Arkansas. Stephens formed W.T.I. in January 1980 to build and operate hazardous waste incinerators. East Liverpool was one of its first projects. In 1988 Stephens gave $100,000 to the Republican Party, and he and his wife were hosts to an inaugural bash for President Bush. He also once helped rescue a Harkin Energy project for Bush's son when it was undercapitalized.

As is so often the case, the wealthy wheeler-dealer was adept at working with both major parties:

> In 1992 Stephens, who had earlier supported Bill Clinton in his Arkansas races, raised $100,000 for him and extended a $3.5 million line of credit to his campaign through the Worthen Bank, which is partly owned by the Stephens family. The Clinton campaign deposited up to $55 million in federal election funds in this bank.

136

The White House of "the Middle Class"

> The conflicts of interest don't stop there. The man now ultimately responsible for E.P.A. decisions on W.T.I. is Deputy Administrator Robert Sussman, a law school classmate of Bill and Hillary Clinton. Sussman previously acted as legal counsel to the Chemical Manufacturing Association, at a time when two of its biggest clients, Du Pont and BASF, were negotiating contracts to supply two-thirds of the waste to W.T.I. He also represented chemical manufacturers in a lawsuit involving enforcement of the federal Toxic Substances Control Act.

The W.T.I. saga is yet another reminder of how easily campaign promises can be betrayed. But Bill Clinton and Al Gore, as individuals, are not very significant. Their behavior, after all, is part of a pervasive pattern—with the personal qualities of a politician mattering much less than the dominant system of economic power. That system has little to fear from the fantasy that we can safeguard ecological balance by electing "good" people.

As autumn 1993 began, I asked the editor of *Earth Island Journal* for his overall evaluation of Clinton's policies affecting the environment. Gar Smith responded in a way that typified the ambivalence of many environmentalists:

> Bill Clinton may be the best we'll ever get from government. He has taken some major risks and deserves credit for many accomplishments that would have been inconceivable under the Reagan and Bush administrations, but he still represents a divided constituency. People want jobs, industry wants profits, and the biosphere doesn't vote (unless you count floods, droughts and holes in the ozone layer). Clinton's style of

137

government by compromise has set us on the road to a kinder, gentler apocalypse. Clinton's standing in the middle of the road, trying to find common ground between two enormous forces moving in opposite directions—unchecked growth and life itself. Unfortunately, these forces do share a common ground—Planet Earth—and that fact puts them on a collision course. Clinton accepts the premise that economic growth and a consumer society are in fact sustainable. But a sustainable job would be based on enduring natural cycles, not on the one-time extraction of limited resources. Clinton has a technocrat's vision of the future—not a Garden of Eden but a Silicon Valley. It is appalling that Clinton would embrace Free Trade, which is simply applying the discredited rich-man's fantasy of trickle-down economics on a global scale.

During 1993, Alexander Cockburn wrote many columns exposing ugly realities beneath the White House eco-hype; at the end of summer he observed that Interior Secretary Bruce Babbitt "threatens to achieve victories over environmentalists that the Reagan and Bush administrations never dared dream of, amid reverential treatment from a press corps that hails him as the scion of John Muir." A long-awaited Democratic president has implemented a liberal mode of allowing corporations to contaminate air, water, and soil. The rationales and the effects are familiar: corporate profits and ecological destruction.

But, after all, why should nature be exempt from lucrative plans for the world? As Doug Henwood writes in the introduction to this book, the

The White House of "the Middle Class"

North American Free Trade Agreement is part of "the bipartisan free-trade agenda, which holds that the entire globe should be a free-fire zone for multinational capital." The strong support for that agenda from both President Bush and President Clinton reflects their shared commitment to serving the bottom-line interests of huge corporations. In the words of economics professor Melvin Burke, "NAFTA is, in fact, little more than the latest strategy of orthodox economists and conservative politicians to redistribute income and wealth from the many to the few and from the poorest to the richest countries and classes." Is that what you were hoping for when Clinton became president?

Seven

Liberal Haze and the Centrist Dream

One hot afternoon in the middle of 1968, I visited Resurrection City in Washington. Martin Luther King Jr. was dead, buried only a couple of months earlier. I was sixteen, a kid from the suburbs, hearing stories of chaotic despair in the encampment and seeing the disarray of tents marooned in deep mud from the summer rains. What was left of the Poor People's Campaign was falling into a gloomy sinkhole of history. The inhabitants of Resurrection City, and the millions they represented, could wait. And wait. And wait. Definitely, they could wait. Indefinitely.

In the five years since King had come out with a book titled *Why We Can't Wait,* the civil rights movement's demands that would cost the government little in dollars, such as anti-discrimination laws and voting rights, had gained enormous ground—but the emerging demands for economic justice were getting nowhere. Nationwide, intractable conditions required a critique of the jobs performed not by Southern police chiefs but by bankers and slumlords and investors and corporate magnates of the

North, South, East and West. Few of the movers and shakers in mainstream politics were ever interested in disrupting the cash flow of big-time profit-takers. Plus, there was a war on, and with the U.S. government's military spending on the rise for warfare in Indochina, conventional liberalism was blinkered at the water's edge. The vice president, HHH, was a symbol of liberals who stood behind policies causing many more deaths—in faraway villages with military attention and in urban ghettos with calculated neglect—than the toll ever taken by KKK nightriders.

"The bombs in Vietnam explode at home; they destroy the hopes and possibilities for a decent America," King said. He added: "We must combine the fervor of the civil rights movement with the peace movement. We must demonstrate, teach and preach, until the very foundations of our nation are shaken." With such talk, in early 1967, King fully excommunicated himself from the theo-political confines of hazy liberalism. He unequivocally renounced the Vietnam War at a time when doing so made him a premature anti-militarist. King was giving voice to his anguish about the war; he was also responding to the examples set by some activists who had been quicker to openly oppose the war (and were trashed by the press as a result). When King spoke out, his message was clear. "A nation that continues year after year to spend more money on military defense than on programs of social uplift is approaching spiritual death."

In these Clinton days—when institutional violence may be less overt but the consequences of presidential policy are no less profound in terms of human life—we would do well to remember how out of bounds King was, when he took on the Democrat in the White House. A president with a fine civil rights record. A political friend. So much better than the Republicans.

King was all the more threatening to the nation's power structure because he linked ongoing and grievous injustices, domestic and international, encompassing class and race. "A true revolution of values will soon look uneasily on the glaring contrast of poverty and wealth," King told an audience on April 4, 1967, exactly 365 days before he died. His call for *a true revolution of values* was far from abstract: "With righteous indignation, it will look across the seas and see individual capitalists of the West investing huge sums of money in Asia, Africa and South America, only to take the profits out with no concern for the social betterment of the countries, and say: 'This is not just.' It will look at our alliance with the landed gentry of Latin America and say: 'This is not just.' The Western arrogance of feeling that it has everything to teach others and nothing to learn from them is not just." And King spoke about "reordering our priorities, so that the pursuit of peace will take precedence over the pursuit of war."

Race, we've been told lately, is "our national obsession." But I wonder if it isn't also our national evasion—which may explain why America's so-called "race problem" remains so massive. It's really about the huge obstacles to "reordering our priorities." It's about power and wealth and privilege, and the system that sustains them.

These are matters of life and death. A quarter-

143

century after Resurrection City disappeared, in mid-1993, the federal government's National Center for Health Statistics reported a death rate several times higher for the poor than for the affluent. The difference has become more extreme in recent decades. "Among various income groups, the degree of inequality in mortality rates more than doubled from 1960 to 1986," said the epidemiologist in charge of the study, Dr. Gregory Pappas. "The gap between the mortality rate for blacks and the rate for whites has widened over the last ten years, and we knew that was happening. But we found that the class gap is also widening. The disparity between the death rates of high-income blacks and low-income blacks has increased. So has the gap between high- and low-income whites."

Those gaps couldn't be explained simply by unequal access to medical care, said an editorial in the *New England Journal of Medicine,* noting that "socioeconomic status is a powerful determinant of health." The *New York Times* summarized the study's findings, among people twenty-five to sixty-four years old in the United States, this way: "The death rate for white men with family income of less than $9,000 a year was 6.7 times the rate for white men with income of $25,000 or more. For white women in the lower income group, the death rate was 4.1 times that of white women in the higher income group. Among poorer black men, the death rate was 5.4 times the rate for black men in the higher income group. The death rate of poor black women was 3.3 times that of affluent black women." And as for adults, so with the young; the death rates of children vary sharply, according to race and financial bracket.

More than one out of five children now lives below the official poverty line in the U.S.; for black children the figure is 45 percent. Even such statistics are understatements. In 1989, the congressional Joint Economic Committee issued a report saying that 58 million Americans—nearly a quarter of the entire population—should be considered impoverished, taking into account changes in economic conditions since the poverty line was defined in the 1960s.

II

One hot afternoon in the middle of 1993, on a commuter train outside Chicago, two young African-Americans were talking about the authorities in a nearby city. One said: "Why do they hate black people?"

"I don't know," came the reply. "Only God knows that."

Eavesdropping across the aisle, at that instant I wished that I could crawl out of my white skin. Maybe I was guilty of nothing—but I felt implicated, nonetheless. At the time I didn't think of Resurrection City, but later those moments on the train seemed similar to a quarter-century earlier, leaving the muddy impasse not far from the Lincoln Memorial and going home.

White people commonly know much more about racism than they're willing to acknowledge. Shielded from a barrage of subtle and overt racial bias that falls elsewhere every day, they are aware—somewhere in their hearts—that the heavy weight of history is a massive burden for many other people

145

in the present day.

But whites usually find it convenient to pretend that the past is mere prologue. James Baldwin called this "the fraudulent and expedient nature of the American innocence which has always been able to persuade itself that it does not know what it knows too well." We cling to the pseudo-innocence, as if by doing so we absolve ourselves of culpability for dodging other people's pain.

Today the cumulative despair of poverty and unequal opportunity is pervasive among African-Americans and Latinos and Native Americans—people largely unconcerned with glass ceilings because they are trapped below the economic floorboards. Meanwhile, many Asian immigrants are over-whelmed by racism and cultural upheaval. And millions of whites are among the country's destitute.

The arrival of a new president in 1993 con-firmed, again, that acceptance of poverty is, in practice, bipartisan. While federal programs promise to ameliorate, pitiful budgets guarantee that they won't have much impact. Fervent words and occasional speeches from top Democrats, however heartfelt at the moment, count for little more than elaborate cosmetics.

With huge gaps between rich and poor accepted as normal, even empathetic news reports about poor children avoid ascribing their plights to govern-ment policy decisions. Among many pundits and politicians, cutbacks of "welfare" programs are apt to be portrayed as frugal and even courageous stands against "special interests" and "entitle-ments." Female heads of households, making do with scant resources, are fair game for the vitriol that lacquers so much discussion of "welfare reform"; millions of women, noble in their efforts to nurture children and keep families together, are made the objects of resentment, innuendo and derision. Meanwhile, tacitly or explicitly, the poor—especially black people—are often blamed for their own dire situations. Moralizers who wield the spotlight of blame are adept at eluding its glare. When *Newsweek* senior editor Joe Klein wrote in 1993 that "out-of-wedlock births to teenagers are at the heart of the nexus of pathologies that define the underclass," there was no mention of white racism as any kind of pathology at all.

Condemnation of violent street crime is rarely coupled with denunciation of institutional violence—the sort that leaves so many youngsters without access to adequate health care or nutrition, decent housing or education or employment...in short, without access to a future. When the budget pies get sliced, all the egalitarian rhetoric in the world is beside the point. And when white people sustain old priorities, a brutal past lives on in the present. We may say that the past is in the past—that today we hate no one—but our actions and inaction tell a different story.

III

Six months into the Clinton presidency, the *New York Times* reported on a nationwide poll of Ross Perot supporters commissioned by the Democratic Leadership Council—which the *Times* described as "a centrist group that was a base for Mr. Clinton's presidential campaign." The tenth paragraph of the article included, in passing, this sentence: "Al From, the president of the Democratic Leadership Council, said Mr. Clinton had an opportunity to form a governing majority just as President Richard M. Nixon did when he followed a 'Southern strategy' to win support from disaffected Democrats who had voted for George Wallace in 1968."

The analogy was especially chilling because of what it managed to say and not say at the same time. It implied deferring to prejudice—racism, in fact—yet it retained deniability, couched in terms of swing votes and historical parallels of voting blocs alienated from both major political parties. Nixon's "Southern strategy" itself had been paved with denial; Tricky Dick said emphatically in the mid-1960s that it would be wrong for the Republican Party to court racist white votes—votes he went on to court assiduously in his successful presidential campaigns.

Al From's comment should have caused an uproar in the national press. Instead it was taken in stride as hardball politics. And why not? The Democratic Party had won the presidency while lassoing some voters who'd eluded them for a while, and nothing succeeds like success. Clinton's key targets, as Manning Marable wrote on the eve of the election, included "'Reagan Democrats,' the white, blue-collar workers who abandoned the party of Roosevelt and Kennedy over affirmative action, busing for school desegregation, and welfare."

Noting what was obvious to many blacks and opaque for all too many whites about the Clinton-Gore effort, political scientist Adolph Reed Jr. observed that "the campaign has sent out very disturbing signals, particularly in its carefully coded pandering to white racism." Mondale in '84 and Dukakis in '88 "were not exactly fiery champions of equality and social democracy. But this ticket's commitment to retreat from social justice is militant where the others were tepid. Their two predecessors drifted rightward; the Confederate Twins steer enthusiastically. They represent the victory of the DLC, the organizational embodiment of the party's Southern, white, male wing that has fought against every progressive initiative since the New Deal."

And Herbert Hill, a professor of Afro-American studies, put it this way: Clinton's campaign was "based on an appeal to the white vote, North and South, while ignoring the most vital interests of the African-American and other nonwhite communities.... The rage against white racism among African-Americans and other minority groups is very deep, and the cities are now potential battlefields of violent and disastrous racial conflict. But Clinton has no civil-rights program. He has, in fact, failed to address concretely the issue of racism, and instead has made every effort to distance himself from civil-rights advocates."

On his presidential trail, Bill Clinton got into the rhythm of a balancing act, postured forward on civil rights when convenient, while riding a back-lash. Quite a few speeches that helped gain him the nomination (particularly as he made the rounds of party officials in 1991) were filled with assertions that people on welfare should be required to prove themselves worthy of government aid—"rhetoric of 'personal responsibility' conspicuously addressed only to black audiences," as Adolph Reed described the standard Clinton lingo. No such ultimatums were fired in the direction of polluting and otherwise irresponsible corporations. Another Southern pol present at the creation of the Democratic Leadership Council, close Clinton ally Charles Robb, had been explicit back in the middle 1980s when the DLC was formed: "It's time to shift the primary focus from racism, the traditional enemy from without, to self-defeating patterns of behavior, the new enemy within."

That kind of talk was hailed by many a political analyst as evidence of new maturity among some up-and-coming Democrats. Those same analysts lauded Clinton for his efforts to distance the national Democratic Party from poor people failing to behave as they should. Focusing on "behavior," Clinton implied that quite a few people getting assistance were taking advantage of federal, state, and local agencies: "If we are going to be the party of government...we can't have people think we are captives of our own bureaucracy and that we don't recognize any responsibility on the part of the people who benefit from government programs to give something back in terms of responsible behavior," he said in a standard speech in mid-1991. While Clinton displayed a far more lenient attitude toward the powerful, he frequently demanded "responsible behavior" from people lacking power.

"We're going to empower people to take control of their own lives, then hold them accountable for doing so," Clinton proclaimed. In a keynote address to the DLC's national convention in May 1991, he maintained that "if we give opportunity without insisting on responsibility, much of the money can be wasted and the country's strength can still be sapped. So we favor responsibility for all. That's the idea behind national service. It's the idea behind welfare reform." Did he say "if we *give opportunity*"? Yes indeed. Lost in the verbal shuffle, in all the riffs about "responsible behavior," was the principle that real opportunity is a right, not a gift.

The final draft of the 1992 party platform was a triumph for ascendant Democrats—young, gifted and white—reveling in media accolades for their "moderate" fusion of disparate party elements. But their victory was a loss for Americans getting burned at the bottom of the melting pot. The Democratic platform's emphasis on voluntarism instead of government programs suggested that the document could have been entitled "Five Hundred Points of Light." Or perhaps "G.O.P. Lite." When the platform rejected "the big government theory that says we can hamstring business and tax and spend our way to prosperity," the buzz-phrases seemed recycled from decades of Republicanism—exempting a bloated Pentagon from the "big government" tag, and echoing the Grand Old Party's denunciations of what all governments must do—"tax and spend." The public sector was to be squeezed hard, in a process that along the way codified such rhetoric as new themes for the national Democratic Party.

"Moderate" was the plaudit of choice conferred on the '92 Democratic Convention and its platform. But for many people, the new and improved party centrism had ominous implications. For tens of millions in the United States, there was nothing moderate about economic distress. Even if George Bush were ousted from the White House, how much difference would that make for them?

IV

Clichés are enemies of meaning. Yet political clichés are not meaningless—they are instruments and results of methodical calculations. By harping on individual "responsibility" and "behavior," Clinton seemed committed to reshaping the Democratic Party to frame such concepts as political goals more pressing than social justice and equal opportunity. In effect, ritual platitudes aside, many of his political lectures were cool to people still suffering the effects of past and present discrimination. The new party platform told people reeling from deprivation that they'd need to behave properly in order to benefit from government programs. But what about the corporations that—to put it mildly—benefit from government policies? The New Democrats, busy endorsing corporate America's checks, had few unkind words for them.

The '92 Democratic Convention confirmed that corporate interests had gained more bipartisan dominance than ever. But news media focused on relatively powerless grassroots groups as threats to Democratic Party "unity." When eminent think-tanker Norman Ornstein looked up from hors d'oeuvres and told me midway through the convention that "poor people don't do very much," it was a hope as well as a judgment. From a centrist vantage point, modern pluralism should balance but not negate the divine right of king-sized capital to circumscribe society's options with the enormous clout of class power; the natural order includes immense leverage wielded by the wealthy, and debilitating inertia suffered by people who live from paycheck to paycheck, or welfare check to welfare check, or no check at all. Meanwhile, the New Democrats were hardly about to upset any big-money apple carts.

And yet, once nominated, there were many good reasons to vote for Clinton and Gore, to defeat their Republican opponents. "And so I will choose two of the four white men," June Jordan wrote. "Two of them have not yet proven themselves inhumane and besotted by fantasies of faraway conquest. Two of them have attempted to speak about trees and jobs and the rich. Two of them have yet to go on public record against the necessity and the preservation of public education. Two of them apparently regard national health care as a desirable entitlement rather than a neo-communist threat. Two of them have yet to veto civil-rights legislation. Two of them espouse a woman's right to abortion."

But after the elation of seeing Bush and Quayle evicted from their tax-funded homes in Washington, it was sobering to see how little change was in the offing. Anyone heartened by Clinton's election-year talk about wanting to aid urban America, for instance, was due for a harsh reality check within months of his inauguration. By summer 1993 the cities—with millions of residents remaining mired in abysmal conditions—had gotten the message from the new team at the White House.

"Mayors, who were clamoring for more federal assistance earlier this year, now say that their expectations from Washington have diminished," the *New York Times* reported. *Newsweek* declared that for the nation's mayors "the futility of complaint has become obvious: there will be no significant help for them from Washington, not even from a president who understands their problems, feels their pain and—more to the point—probably couldn't have been elected without their support."

Typically, the Democrat serving as head of the National League of Cities, Minneapolis mayor Donald Fraser, was willing to swallow the disappointment and make excuses: "We're getting more understanding of our problems and greater willingness to help from the Clinton administration. But they are severely constrained by the budget deficit they inherited." Somehow that deficit hadn't prevented the same administration's huge outlays for the Pentagon. It all came down, as usual, to *priorities.* And inner-city poor people—mostly black and Latino—weren't.

Clinton's basic economic program was in place by late summer 1993, dishing out more of the same to the downtrodden. "The administration's proud budget bill could have been pushed just as easily by a Republican president," remarked Emory Curtis, a columnist for the black-run *California Voice* newspaper based in San Francisco. He added:

> The administration has bought the Republican definition of economic progress—a healthy stock market and profitable companies...
>
> The Congressional Black Caucus used its muscle in budget negotiations and got a $2.5 billion expansion of the food stamp program, about $600 million for free childhood immunizations, $1 billion for family welfare programs and $3.5 billion for empowerment and enterprise zones. Relatively, the total wasn't much but, without the Caucus, the total could have been much lower.
>
> The enterprise and empowerment zone concepts are the administration's new thrust for

economic development of depressed areas. It is a Republican idea; Jack Kemp, a former Republican congressman, pushed enterprise zones for the past ten years or so. However, at best, the authorization contains only enough funds to test the concepts of empowerment and enterprise zones; there is not enough for a real attack on urban area economic problems....

President Clinton is pushing for $3.4 billion to pay for 50,000 more police officers on the streets. This makes dollars for police the Clinton administration's central urban initiative.

It was a vicious irony that twenty-four years earlier, an incoming president had received a key memorandum that could have fit neatly on Clinton's desk in the Oval Office. Written to Richard Nixon just prior to his inauguration in January 1969, the memo from Daniel Patrick Moynihan advised that "the time may have come when the issue of race could benefit from a period of benign neglect." Moynihan argued for "trying to create some equivalence between what Government can do about certain problems and how much attention it draws to them." Clinton's pals at the Democratic Leadership Council couldn't have said it more succinctly.

V

With its eyes on the presidential prize in the 1990s, the DLC's main objective "was an attack on the Democratic Party's core constituencies—labor, schoolteachers, women's rights groups, peace and disarmament activists, the racial minorities and supporters of affirmative action," William Greider said in his book *Who Will Tell the People.* "Its stated goal was to restore the party's appeal to disaffected white males, especially in the South, but the DLC discussions did not focus on the economic decline afflicting those citizens. Instead, it promoted the notion that Democrats must distance themselves from the demands of women or blacks or other aggrieved groups within the party. The Reverend Jesse Jackson and his provocative economic agenda aimed at workers, white and black, was a favorite target of the Democratic Leadership Council and, on Capitol Hill, the DLC was sometimes waggishly referred to as 'the white boys' caucus.'"

At the start of the decade, Greider saw the Democratic Party as "divided by nasty ideological combat between the party's Washington elites and its rank-and-file constituencies—the people at the grassroots who are most active in Democratic politics. The establishment's quarrel was with the party's own voters. The people they belittled as 'activists' and 'interest groups' were the very people who cared most intensely about public issues and who formed the faithful core of the party's electorate, win or lose. The Democratic establishment did not wish to initiate a dialogue with these citizens, only to make them go away or at least keep their mouths shut." After 1992, that establishment controlled not only the national party but also the White House. Its power, and its arguments, could seem even stronger—for inducing people with more progressive desires to (now more than ever) "keep their mouths shut."

Curbing expectancy is part of the campaign cycle—and one of the insidious things about presidential campaigns is that they never end. There is always another election coming up, with ample rationales for doing what shouldn't be done and for not doing what should. Deference to "realism"—as defined by a status quo bound up in corporate biases—is always applicable for the next election.

In the spring of 1992, *Newsweek* took warm note of candidate Clinton's steady "middle course," adding: "Conscious of the need to avoid kowtowing to liberal Democratic interest groups, he has largely avoided making promises to labor, ethnic and minority groups." Six months later, as the fall campaign got underway, the magazine's staff columnist Joe Klein extolled the DLC as "the party's most intellectually adventurous group"—the kind of hype widespread in news media busily celebrating old centrist wine in new bottles, nearly full for corporate interests and mostly empty for others.

Writing in the *Progressive* magazine that autumn, Manning Marable laid out the grim picture: "After a decade of Reaganism, the political cultures of both major parties have shifted decisively to the right. It was in this context of reaction that Clinton and the conservative cabal, the Democratic Leadership Council, seized control of the party's national apparatus. Their conservative agenda represents a sharp break from the New Deal-Great Society liberalism." For decades, that liberalism had given little reason for rejoicing, and many reasons for grief; but things could have been worse, and now they were. A campaign commercial told TV viewers in October 1992: "They're a new generation of Democrats—Bill Clinton and Al Gore. And they don't think the way the old Democratic Party did." As if echoing the cogent words of toe-tapping Bob Roberts, the national Democratic Party had gone a long way toward adopting a new anthem for itself: "The times they are a-changin' back"—but, of course, in an intellectually adventurous way.

The advantages of Clinton-style centrism have been clear and real enough for the powerful who wish to remain so. Nationally, in 1992, the G.O.P. was tarred with an economic mess and swimming in the deep-end of a fundamentalist cesspool on the right. If the White House pendulum had to swing away from Reagan-Bush extremes, then Clintonism was ideal for defining the other end of the swing for corporate America. ("Fiscal conservatism and social liberalism.")

For people wanting political change of a progressive sort, warm feelings toward the young president were usually in the context of his being obviously "better than the Republicans"—but as the Clinton administration settled into power, its apparent virtues thinned on their merits. When people who had despised Reagan and Bush, for all the left reasons, tried to understand what President Clinton was up to, they were increasingly faced with choosing between discontent and delusion. Several months after Clinton's inauguration, the new president could only be admired from the left with credulity bordering on the hallucinogenic; his virtues were, for the most part, mirages, floating across TV screens and web-fed pages, imitating horizons, fulfilling a few modest hopes and foreclosing many others.

VI

The "moderate" Democratic Party of the 1990s has been succeeding at the politics of evasion, avidly competing in the big national marketplace where denial is sought and bold. If we want to feel good about ourselves as compassionate people and we are somehow ambivalent about challenging the cruel underbelly of American privilege, Clintonism may be the flavor of the decade. Some real advances could be identified—yet they would predictably mean little to many millions of people whose lives were bleak and prospects bleaker. To feel good or even equivocal about President Clinton would require not looking too hard at the daily predicaments of others who may seem real but not *too* real, whose lives could be tacitly bypassed, left in excruciating limbo or worse.

To accept the mirage of a humanistic Clinton administration, it helps—enormously—to be white and not poor. Tens of millions of people living outside those categories in this country are still shunted aside by the nation's capital. The poor are still lashed to the shell of snail's-pace gradualism that Martin Luther King Jr. denounced as totally unacceptable when the Poor People's Campaign was launched—nonviolently and militantly—with the announced intention of shutting down normal operations of the federal government, at a time when a "war on poverty" had slipped from the presidential agenda. Now, more than twenty-five years later, with another Democrat in the White House, a real challenge to poverty cannot be found anywhere on that agenda. From the fallow fields of abandonment and betrayal symbolized by Resurrection City, the harvest of Democratic moderation is bitter.

While dismal implications stretch to the eternity of a lifetime for some, for others the suffering can only be secondhand—vicarious, and optional. Political patience is a virtue that comes easiest to those with the least immediate pain and the most options—the "virtuous" who can appreciate the nuances of pragmatic accommodation. It is perhaps impolite (but useful) to say that the tenor of your "politics" is likely to have a great deal to do with where you wake up in the morning—at issue here is tone and urgency more than espoused ideals or self-description—because a sense of urgency tends to be inversely proportional to economic security and social advantage. Inclination to see the bright side of patient realism is apt to be diminished if you are not sure how you will pay the rent next month, if the house-hold surroundings are shabby and not by choice, if the color of your skin subjects you to indignities great and small in a country where the hue of epidermis can affect so much on the street and in a life.

Bill Clinton understands well that much of American liberalism, white and far from poor, is patient to a fault, and thus is prone to mush into feeling O.K. about centrism. With good intentions—but with more fidelity to comforting illusions than to the value of mobilizing behind their best dreams—people can be lulled, and lulled again; a drowsy ambience is enhanced and reinforced by mass media in day-to-day sync with politicians. Every so-called "moderate" on Capitol Hill is part of the extremism of the great American political middle—George Mitchell to Bob Dole, Sam Donaldson to George Will—a spectrum made to seem reasonable and wide-ranging through power and repetition. *Moderate* is the ultimate compliment for a system constantly re-establishing its genteel and brutal bearings.

Routine language reflects aversion to clarity. Unseemly political control holds up a mirror to itself and endlessly exclaims at the democratic beauties in the looking glass. "Moderate" is one of the linguistic cosmetics applied not so much to ourselves as to the mirrors we hold up for ourselves, and for each other, groggy and accustomed to the disingenuous. Honesty is precious and scarce not because we abstractly prefer to hide from difficult truths, but because we so often gauge life to be easier when we avoid candor. In the process, "linguicide" is among the mechanisms of psychological incarceration, rendering freedoms (of speech and action) largely unused, theoretical and unexplored, existing only beyond the unseen bars rarely passed through. That way, in an avowedly "free" society, people can readily become their own guards—internalizing and self-censoring—while images of luxury and anguish keep flickering across TV screens, touting political and commercial nostrums to provide hazy soporifics for everyday lives.

I'm O.K., you're O.K.; most of us are O.K.; kind of. The image of majority inclusion is a way for us to join in the shrug. Compromise is in the air, recommended as a two-way street, but the heavy traffic is in one direction, fueled by mega-dollars and routed at the convenience of powers-that-be. What can you do? The answer is available from ninety-seven channels on cable: Not much.

Silence is often the most profound of screaming lies. What endures is adherence to national politics that absolutely relies on deception as a mode of governance.

Eight

Enabling the Status Quo

One day, in 1990, Garrison Keillor gave a speech at San Francisco's prestigious Commonwealth Club. After an amusing monologue about culture and food and gaining weight, he fielded questions. Someone inquired about his current political outlook. There was a weighty pause. He acknowledged feeling more than a little confusion. Certainty was now hard to come by, he went on, given the complex events of the just-passed decade.

Some listeners waited in anticipation of more. But there *was* no more. And there was no danger that anybody in the well-heeled audience would choke on an after-lunch cigar or become otherwise apoplectic, no reason to worry that the hosts would find their speaker bad for digestion. Next question?

Keillor's presentation was being broadcast to radio listeners all over Northern California and beyond. Since food had been a theme of his speech, he might have said something, for instance, about the contrast between the wealthy elite who had just finished an opulent meal and the many homeless only blocks away. But confusion was better. Numbed silence was better. Maybe he wanted to be invited back. Maybe he wanted the audience to like him.

163

Maybe... One can speculate as to motives. But the results were more empirical: Garrison Keillor had been asked to say something of substance. In reply, he said that he was confused. And in those moments, he contributed to the further numbing of America.

Keillor was replicating the fuzziness that customarily prevails with reference to politics and power in daily life. Whatever is understood privately, little is discussed openly about dynamics of leverage and suppression: in a family, or in a relationship, or in the workplace, or in the country as a whole. No need to get too heavy, or make people too uneasy.

Heard on hundreds of public stations each weekend, Keillor's regular radio program is a popular variety show invoking home and hearth with a little hipness thrown in. The show appeals to an audience that ranges wide; it's a perfect crossover production—a weekly source of sweet tunes and gentle mockery, safe and tinged with daring at the same time, offensive only to those who mind the recurrent spoofing of old-style Lutherans in the Mid-West. Supplying irreverence that can be mistaken for substantive dissent, Keillor's broadcast could be understood as a diluted radio analog to the naughty antics of Bart Simpson.

In 1992, a teacher at an Iowa community college—who expressed vehement political views akin to Pat Robertson's—told me that he loved to watch "The Simpsons." It was, he said without reservation, a terrific show. Many a leftist might agree. A witty fast pace provides viewers with a variety of delightful moments, provoking laughter and any number of projected interpretations. But unlike Matt

Groening's "Life in Hell" cartoons that continued to appear in newsprint weeklies around the country, "The Simpsons" became part of the nebulous mass-culture it satirized. When Bart and his family starred in Butterfinger Bar commercials on the tube, it was no joke. When millions of children played the Simpsons video game—featuring plenty of fisticuffs from the family, and Marge bashing people with her vacuum cleaner—the game's protagonists might be mistaken for imitators of Bluto and Popeye and Olive Oyl, transposed to a video display screen. Soaring with commercial success, "The Simpsons" became part of the problem.

The slide into profitable co-option is entangled in social mores; prudence insists that one stay within shouting distance, or perhaps stroking distance, of the center. For the most part, to speak clearly against the ruthlessness of power in our midst would be tacky, gauche, impolite...and hardly shrewd. The propriety of covering one's ass becomes a kind of social Thorazine. Fixations on (selected) injustice far away often substitute for hard looks at what is happening closer to home. Attacks on the ersatz become ersatz themselves.

Mass media are adept at deluging authentic concerns with watered-down products. So, with an environmental crisis all around us, the most widely promoted "solutions" have frequently been little more than innocuous fluff. As the 1990s got underway, one of the flagships lifted by waves of Earth Day hype was the slim book *50 Simple Things You Can Do to Save the Earth*, which sold more than 3.5 million copies within a year—amid much praise as a harbinger of ecological awareness for the mainstream. Carefully edited to avoid offending any corporation guilty of pollution, the book stuck to tepid recycling-type suggestions. Soon it spun off into a second manual, *50 Simple Things Kids Can Do to Save the Earth.* The new publishing house Earthworks Press was carving out a respectable niche under a superficial save-the-earth crust.

"Our third book was our first major premium," says an Earthworks brochure. And what better initial client for an environmental publisher than a nuclear-power-invested utility? "Working with Pacific Gas & Electric, the nation's largest utility, we created *30 Simple Energy Things You Can Do to Save the Earth.* It has been used by twenty-six different utilities. Since then, Earthworks has produced millions of customized books for businesses and government agencies. We've created special editions for Kodak, Nabisco, Clorox, Shaklee, Tambrands, Wells Fargo [Bank], and dozens more." A customized book, the Earthworks pitch goes on, "identifies your company with genuinely useful information.... Links your name with Earthworks' high standards and reputation.... The Earthworks Group guarantees to help you design a book that effectively appeals to your specific audience and reflects your specific mission."

The same year that Earthworks neo-ecology books were topping paperback bestseller lists, *Newsweek* drama critic Jack Kroll was writing that "the American social conscience seems inert or baffled by the problems of a more complex time." Part of being baffled is, as George Orwell observed, refusal to acknowledge that one is playing dumb—or that others are also doing so. Social issues often are abstracted because to be specific could be uncomfortable; it's easier to defer to our "complex time" than to risk inconvenience or worse. Fogginess surrounds. Complexity serves as a continual excuse: *Everything's so complicated, I've got nothing adamant to say* (a paraphrase of Garrison Keillor at the Commonwealth Club's dais, circa 1990). Equivocation seems preferable to strong and unsettling conviction, dismissed as appropriate for another era or another land.

II

Many people are thankful that the president who took office in 1993 is not a right-wing Republican. (Many others can appreciate, equally, that he is not a left-wing Democrat.) Winning points by disparaging "stale ideologies," Bill Clinton has repackaged centrist ideology to make it seem relatively fresh. Weary of the tedious polemical strife that persisted while the country deteriorated, we may be drawn to what appears to be practical—a middle ground that displeases the political extremes while creating more social cohesion and getting some positive things accomplished.

In August 1993, *In These Times* published an irate letter from Utah: "Listen! Bill Clinton is our knight in shining armor. Unlike dream candidates that we all love, this one gets elected, can raise money to get elected and does get some things done." And an irate letter from California: "Do you want Republicans back in '96? Clinton's not far enough left for you? As an elderly leftie, I'll make do with young Mr. Clinton at this point." And an irate letter from Minnesota: "I'm offended at your attacks on Clinton. What you say may be true, but there's a lot you don't say that is also true. I'd like to see *In These Times* give support and recognition for efforts by the president to hold our country together. If liberals cut him down, then what? Dole or Perot? Don't help destroy what could be a little hope, please."

Much of big media goodwill toward Clinton can be traced to his tones of moderation—in contrast to polarization that *New York Times* critic Michiko Kakutani has ascribed, in part, to "ideologues on either end of the political spectrum imposing their paint-by-the-numbers formulations on the national debate." In the early summer of 1993, Kakutani's condemnation of strident passions appeared atop the front page of the *Times* "Living Arts" section, under the headline "Against the Tide: Making a Case for Shades of Gray." Articulating an aesthetic of measured response rather than heated advocacy, Kakutani echoed themes that had been sounded for years in the political news pages. Being close to the center line, it was easy to see how out of bounds some contestants could be: "Conservatives remember the '60s, when they saw liberals as obscenity-shouting radicals; liberals remember the '80s, when they saw conservatives as greedy capitalist pigs." And today, "an assortment of domestic bogeymen have been proposed by ideologues on both the left and right." On the subject of ideologues of the center, Kakutani's long essay had nothing to say.

Propaganda from the center commonly casts itself as badly needed perspicacity, a bastion of rationality above the mean-spirited fray. What better way to flack for the status quo than to downplay its horrors and lump all its vehement foes together?

Enabling the Status Quo

To moderate ears, the extremists are exaggerators who often sound remarkably alike, no matter who they are or what they represent.

"In the escalating war of words, hyperbole flourishes, as both sides play to the public's fears, searching for easy scapegoats and convenient straw men," Kakutani wrote. "Extremes consequently begin to dominate the debate: while the left tries to equate conservatives with Jesse Helms, the right tries to equate liberals with Jesse Jackson." Also regrettable is "the tendency to look at all art—both past and present—through an ideological lens." And alas, even the study of history is beset by "the loudest voices" that are "shrill, admitting little room for rational discussion or common sense. Columbus is either the heroic explorer who opened the gates of the New World or the barbaric imperialist who initiated the rape of Eden." Along the way, "When opinions calcify into hard-line stands, when extremists on the right and left define the agenda, the middle ground is lost, and along with it, the possibility of consensus."

But what do these sober-sounding words mean? Where was *the middle ground* or *the possibility of consensus* in earlier times? During slavery? During the suffragist battle for women's right to vote? While Nazis built concentration camps? During the civil rights movement? The Vietnam War?... What was the middle ground? Reduction of slavery? Allowing certain women to vote? Capping the number of death camps? (Auschwitz O.K., but Buchenwald not O.K.?) Desegregate the buses but not the lunch counters? End the air war over Laos and Cambodia, but keep dropping bombs on

Vietnam?... What would the possibility of consensus entail, other than acceding to enormous cruelties of institutionalized violence?

There's a lot to recommend the pursuit of incremental progress that can get things done—a pursuit often seen as feasible, coolheaded, and respectable—in pleasant contrast to what it is *not:* disreputable, marginal, "ideological," radical. Staying away from such designations can seem to be a requirement for being taken seriously, and for being effective. But political centrism—with its liberal and conservative wings—is little more than refurbishment of what already holds sway in the United States. Conditioned to take the nod from what is touted as realism—to shy away from questioning the assumptions of big-ticket politics—we participate in processes that are stultifying our lives, hushing unauthorized voices because they might devalue the social currency of acceptance, security, "success."

Liberalism is a wonderful dream, baited with manifest benefits. But in the United States, liberalism has a tendency to see much of the world as a big Rorschach blot; the vision comes to supersede the shape of everyday life, with convenient projection and denial apt to be mistaken for pragmatism or idealism.

Dreams of a marriage between liberal idealism and centrist pragmatism came to fruition in November 1992. The dozen years of blues had a baby, and its name was Bill Clinton. Brash and smart and wise beyond his years, the young governor had sold himself onto the national stage as a comer who could skip over old political labels and get to the point; in the words of a boilerplate 1991 speech, "We've got to have a message that touches everybody, that makes sense to everybody, that goes beyond the stale orthodoxies of 'left' and 'right.'" The end of ideology was supposed to prefigure an end to rancorous divisions that presumably the society—or at least the Democratic Party—could no longer afford. The New Democrats were insisting, in essence, that the center could be made to hold, for the common good. It was centrist ideology dressed up as anti-ideology—a commitment to adjust the status quo masquerading as a commitment to "change."

Clinton's acclimation to the levers of federal power was larded with symbolism. The first president born after World War Two had gone from '60s idealism to '90s realism—or so we were told, endlessly, by a national press corps heavily staffed with men and women inclined to believe that they themselves had traveled a similar journey to middle-age importance. By early summer 1993, the *Nation* magazine columnist Christopher Hitchens was able to write with full justification about President Clinton's "shabby, gutless performance...presented by the consensus keepers as the turmoil of a closet leftist coming to terms with 'the real world.'" By then, a standard media portrait of President Clinton was that he epitomized the coming-of-age of contemporaries.

The *New York Times* reported in mid-August 1993 that his "pattern reflects two contradictory impulses that Mr. Clinton shares with many members of his generation: idealism and a preference for consensus." With the encouragement of such media spins, millions of people who'd detested Reagan and Bush were getting used to giving Clinton the benefit of their doubts. Thus, Clinton's accommodation becomes a paradigm for our own; his rationales for compromising oft-proclaimed human values become prototypes for our own. And he serves as a new role model for evoking idealism while setting ideals aside in practice—discarding them as though they were remnants of a bygone and less mature era of pimples and principles.

A spirit of reinvention pervaded the convention that nominated Clinton in 1992. Feeling Madison Square Garden shake with Fleetwood Mac's tune "Don't Stop Thinking About Tomorrow," I kept hearing the flip side—the hit single that goes, "Tell me lies, tell me lies, tell me sweet loving lies."

In ongoing attempts to square the spheres of progressive beliefs with centrist boxes, the remolding of words has been helpful. (It's illustrative that when the Democratic Leadership Council set up a think tank in Washington, the name selected was "Progressive Policy Institute.") The emphasis is on being inventive—not in policies so much as in how they are packaged, rationalized, justified and sold. So, if you're concerned about the way this country has been, we'll invent another one for you. No muss, no fuss. During Clinton's first year in the White House, the Democratic National Committee sent out huge mailings that solicited contributions in the $25-$100 range; included in each envelope was a plastic DNC "1993 Contributing Member" card, with a message over Bill Clinton's name: "By accepting this membership card, you will be playing a vital role in reinventing America." A truly appealing

notion—*reinventing America.* With history so routinely evaded and solemnly taught to suit the powerful, why not? Nothing wrong with our nation that
a good "reinventing" can't cure.

III

In recent years, much has been learned and a
lot of insights have been shared about intimate
denial of abuse in families and personal relationships. Efforts to confront the realities of abusive
patterns have often been brave and fruitful; we're
beginning to comprehend the painful effects of out-
rageous abuses—physical and psychological—commonly inflicted on women and young people. We're
learning to stop making excuses for the perpetrators
of abuse in a family.

But what about the denial of abuse in a society? What about the abuse that is routine and "normal," frequently met with a wink or a shrug, or
averted eyes, or silence? The silence around the dinner table of an abusive household is replicated, a
millionfold, on evening news broadcasts. Coming to
terms with an abusive parent or partner is vital; so
is coming to terms with an abusive social order,
enforced by officials in powerful positions. In each
situation, prerequisites for liberation include recog-
nizing what is true, learning to speak it out loud,
and taking action to shatter the denial with words
and deeds, so that more humane possibilities can
be nurtured instead of crushed.

When everyday dynamics of manipulation
remain obscured, the fogginess gets in the way of
people's attempts to improve their lives.
Enhancement of our options, as individuals and as

a society, will depend on exposing power's intricate forms and various methods. Fierce reactions are inevitable.

The first few years of the 1990s saw ferocious media attacks on an array of multicultural activists—widely disparaged as enforcers of "political correctness" for striving to challenge racism, sexism, homophobia and basic monocultural arrogance. The backlash whipped itself into a sustained frenzy. To great mega-media applause, for example, *Time* Magazine's Robert Hughes flayed the "culture of complaint" in his book of the same name; there was little media comment on the irony of this affluent white guy complaining so vociferously and at such length about people who complain. After all, pundits aligned with the powerful don't complain, they *explain.*

The counterattack on vital critiques of power structures was more than simply a defense of existing institutions—it was also a defensive fusillade providing cover for denial of pervasive inequities. In a murky milieu, too much discerning analysis just won't do. We're supposed to be smart enough to know that some things are wrong in society. But we're supposed to be equivocal enough not to openly denounce the underlying imbalances of power; some truths are better left unspoken, especially if they would breach the bounds of proper silence. Yet poet Nikky Finney sums up the consequences: "Silence is not golden. Silence is a very rusty thing. A rusty thing that makes everything around it squeak and stop working."

When some people go to sleep in mansions and others in cardboard boxes; when some people have access to the finest in food, medical care, education and opportunities while others are faced with perennial scarcity; when many human rights atrocities by "friendly" governments are still barely criticized by the White House; when daily large-scale violence against women is not defined as a "crisis" by the agenda-setters of mass media and the federal government; when the grievous wrongs that permeate the society are rarely mentioned in forthright terms by those with the most amplified voices—then consistent *abuse* is an unremitting reality. And the president is a key abuser. No, one person cannot transform the country—but Bill Clinton's actions and inactions are choices, with huge effects. We should not be prettying up a president's chronic evasions; we should not be putting the best face on his calculated failures to speak truthfully about the extent of inequities and the dimensions of injustices, and the human outcomes. We should not rationalize complicity with the imposition of so much human suffering.

As abuse continues, we should not be "enablers"—in a relationship, or in a family, or in a society. (Whatever the context, enablers never lack for reasons to avoid confronting the grim realities: *"Other men are more abusive... We have to be supportive to help him improve... We need to be patient..."*) It is not our responsibility to make excuses for abusers, or to attribute virtue because others are less humane and more cruel. Yet, too often, we accept injurious actions by personal or political "friends" that would be unacceptable if inflicted by other people. We may find comfort in giving the benefit of doubts; politicians are pleased

175

to count on such generosities as they lavish their attention elsewhere.

As in an abusive family, in political America denial is pervasive. If Daddy is an alcoholic, a cruel husband, or a vicious father, others in the family are expected not to say so openly. If the President is maintaining policies that perpetuate abject poverty, his essential decency is to go unchallenged in public.

"Americans," a front-page *New York Times* article reported matter-of-factly in 1993, "have generally regarded presidents as fathers."

IV

In the novel *The Painted Bird,* a young boy wandering in wartime Europe encounters such horrors that he becomes mute. At last, recuperating in a safe haven, he picks up a telephone when it rings next to him. Someone really wants to hear his voice. Suddenly he speaks, in a torrent.

Few of us have been as traumatized as the little boy rendered speechless in Jerzy Kosinski's novel. And today few Americans lack for words. But rarely do we break silence about what has become unspeakable. Enveloped in a dim haze, we carry messages yet to be unsealed. What remains unsaid may be on the tips of our tongues, but those tongues are tied, and flaccid like muscles deprived of exercise. Reluctance has become habit. Usually we do not say what we sense most acutely, do not begin to express what we feel most deeply. What has been routine becomes even more so.

In personal realms, many people have been struggling to overcome longtime shortages of clarity and honesty. Feminist critiques have helped to shine light on previously murky aspects of relationships. And analysis of "dysfunctional" patterns and "codependency" has drawn attention to key truths: Unspoken does not mean unreal; on the contrary, the most debilitating dynamics can go unremarked. Speaking more truthfully is a prerequisite for acknowledging pain and creating some solutions. The process of replacing silence with candor can shatter the molds that have been constricting lives. The benefits come as we break through old constraints.

But many obstacles get in the way of applying those lessons to larger social spheres. In the political economy of denial, there's not much capital behind blunt opposition to systemic abuses of human beings. The deterrents to confrontation are profuse, with towering institutional and financial weight behind them. Emphatic denunciations of dominant power may seem overheated or counterproductive or deranged—but, most of all, imprudent. The main societal rewards are conferred for accommodation. Meanwhile, unexpressed perceptions tend to get buried alive; what could be vibrant ends up stifled.

In a society that places high value on carefully tending to exteriors, appearances can be deceiving, but over time they can't nourish a hungry heart. By now the Organization Man may have appreciable "net worth" but little else; and the offspring, tangled up in ambivalence, are likely to be chafing at binds of their own. For a long time now, cash has been king, a glutinous royalty sealing lips (perhaps even with a kiss!) and enervating inner worlds.

FALSE HOPE

The distances between what we experience and what we assert, what we think and what we say, what we perceive and what we pretend—these are measures of how mute and stultified we have become. Fear need not be sudden terror to be debilitating, immobilizing.

Secreted phones are ringing next to where we lie. Someone really wants to hear what we have to say, what has remained unsaid. It's difficult. But not impossible.

V

We live most days in an uneasy armistice with the status quo, while disquiet roils somewhere inside. Keener insights usually get stuffed, out of sight if not out of mind. The *Encyclopedia Britannica*'s discussion of "cognitive dissonance" is relevant: "The unease or tension that the conflict arouses in a person is relieved by one of several defensive maneuvers: the person rejects, explains away, or avoids the new information, persuades himself that no conflict really exists, reconciles the differences, or resorts to any other defensive means of preserving stability or order in his conception of the world and of himself." In day after day stretching toward a lifetime, what is inflammatory to know must be self-rationed, lest it result in actions breaching the boundaries of the system's apparent tolerance. All too often, numbing has become habit-forming, and a habitat for acquiescence to what should never be accepted.

The human casualties, whether we see them or not, are all around us. And far away. The USA's wars in the Third World come and go, but the priorities and mentalities that they reflect are ongoing. Domestic support for the Gulf War, with its yellow ribbons and massive slaughter in a matter of weeks, was a grisly parallel to the many years when most of U.S. society embraced warfare in Vietnam as necessary unpleasantness. Now, as then, we can get used to just about anything—"our" high-tech firepower taking lives with brilliant proficiency...the deprivation crying out in vain for America to make good on our human possibilities...—while priorities at home and abroad keep reinforcing each other.

Resurrection City has never been mourned, much less resurrected, by the government that demolished it. The violent arrogance behind the Vietnam War has never been renounced by the system that pursued it. Politicians may chalk up Vietnam to past folly, but that war was quintessence, not aberration; in slow motion every annual budget since then has resonated with similar priorities as the United States powers ahead. "We took space back quickly, expensively, with total panic and close to maximum brutality," war correspondent Michael Herr wrote of the U.S. juggernaut in Vietnam. "Our machine was devastating. And versatile. It could do everything but stop."

Whether or not U.S. weaponry is being fired in anger, what Martin Luther King called "the madness of militarism" continues to pillage our social resources. Accompanied by euphemism and denial, the intermittent military warfare in foreign territory has matched constant economic class warfare—from the top down—overseas and in North America. Yet we seem to have few words to describe the extent of the USA's capacities to destroy life while

179

pretending that nothing of the sort is taking place. As Herr put it, the U.S. news media "never found a way to report meaningfully about death, which of course was really what it was all about. The most repulsive, transparent gropes for sanctity in the midst of the killing received serious treatment in the papers and on the air. The jargon of Progress got blown into your head like bullets, and by the time you waded through all the Washington stories and all the Saigon stories, all the Other War stories and the corruption stories and the stories about brisk new gains in ARVN effectiveness, the suffering was somehow unimpressive. And after enough years of that, so many that it seemed to have been going on forever, you got to a point where you could sit there in the evening and listen to the man say that American casualties for the week had reached a six-week low, only eighty GI's had died in combat, and you'd feel like you'd just gotten a bargain."

In the United States, many people feel like they've gotten a bargain when the president is not a Republican. The Democratic administration may seem acceptable, even praiseworthy. But trying to deny or rationalize its brutalities only deepens the tragedies that could have been prevented.

Nine

"The Fierce Urgency of *Now*"

The Democrat in the White House was widely viewed as a friend of civil rights. He'd received the overwhelming majority of black votes across the country, winning the presidential race while defeating the Republican right. Leaders of black groups enjoyed unprecedented access to the inner sanctum of the presidency. He could not do all he wanted to do—budget constraints being what they were—but he was an ally. And he was struggling to guide the nation through a difficult period. Many pragmatic reasons existed to support the president. Unfortunately, as time went on, the president's budget did not sustain hopes for a national effort against poverty. Patience would be necessary.

In contrast to all the rationales for accommodation with the president (who could have been so much worse), reasons for being forthright were singular. "We are now faced with the fact that tomorrow is today," Martin Luther King Jr. declared in 1967, no longer willing to pretend that the forward-looking Southerner in the White House had to be supported despite the costs. "We are confronted with the fierce urgency of *now.* In this unfolding conundrum of life and history there is such a thing as being too late. Procrastination is still the thief of time. Life often leaves us standing bare, naked and dejected with a lost opportunity.... Over the bleached bones and jumbled residues of numerous civilizations are written the pathetic words: 'Too late.' There is an invisible book of life that faithfully records our vigilance or our neglect."

Speaking out, King was heard as a hostile voice—by officials at 1600 Pennsylvania Avenue and by many Democrats elsewhere, uneasy about some presidential policies but much more fearful of the consequences of a lack of unity against the Republicans. King was in direct conflict with the Johnson administration as he insisted, "Our only hope today lies in our ability to recapture the revolutionary spirit and go out into a sometimes hostile world declaring eternal opposition to poverty, racism and militarism.... We still have a choice today: nonviolent coexistence or violent coannihilation."

It will be objected that King was responding to the extraordinary circumstances of the Vietnam War. But his concerns were much more sweeping than that one terrible conflagration. He stressed that violence was also being inflicted every day in other forms and other places—not just by warfare but also by the deadly synergies of poverty's deprivations, racism, and despair. He protested the U.S. government's complicity with the institutional violence of economic injustice, assaulting millions of people in the United States and around the world. In the 1960s, that violence was widespread. Can we honestly say that it is less so in the 1990s? Can we believe that "the fierce urgency of *now*" has become less fierce and less urgent?

II

Overall the Clinton administration reinforces an abusive system, in sync with a broad-based ideology that calls for minor reform accompanied by major rhetoric. The big-money "alternative" to the two-party system—the "United We Stand" bogus populism orchestrated and financed by billionaire Ross Perot—is a dead-end with a megalomaniac for a leader and a deficit-cutting mania for slashing even deeper into government programs that help people. Staying in step with national Democratic Party marching orders may be the lesser of three evils. But, in contrast, a strong progressive movement does not only ask what can be done within current constraints; it also demands to find out how those constraints can be removed, to end the inhuman use of human beings.

The main social gains of the past several decades have resulted directly from activist movements—civil rights, peace, women's rights, environmental, gay rights and others. However, in the absence of a wide analysis of how centralized economic power fuels political power, the mass media and politicians have been able to coopt a lot of social-change energy for the purposes of mild reform and major reinforcement of "the system" as the shepherd for the American flock. Rather than scrutinizing how so many aspects of our lives keep being subjected to corporate domination, the usual public discussion gravitates toward single-issue, personality-laden politics—maintaining a high profile in media, and in the calculations of corporate-backed politicians.

In the national political arena, vital grassroots movements are apt to be handled, blunted, watered-down and siphoned away—while the core of the status quo retains its strength. Instead of political analysis, the fixations have often centered on individual rising-star politicians and their enticing, comet-like myths.

But any particular politicians, and their myths, are disposable. In 1992, Bill Clinton was the "Comeback Kid" who could "take a punch." His efforts to emulate JFK achieved their greatest resonance when he won the presidency. But Clinton got a rough ride from the press in 1993, dimming his political luster; news coverage of *President* Clinton soon combined adulation with a lot of sharp criticism, overbearingly from the right. If he was oft-compared to John F. Kennedy during the successes of 1992, he was—after inauguration in 1993—liable to be likened to Jimmy Carter. No problem. Individual politicians, and mythical parallels, are expendable; they can be cut short as events dictate. The system's loyalty is not to any individual. The president's name changes; the stock exchanges and bond markets endure. Bill Clinton will serve their purposes, more or less, while also serving as a lightning rod for scrutiny that might otherwise focus on the economic powers that maintain themselves no matter who is president.

The never-ending personality parade of politics is a continuous psychodrama that distracts from veiled forces at work. Political leaders respond to power exerted much more by "the fact of oligarchy" than by truly democratic processes. Only when people have organized effectively—with great effort, as in the civil rights and anti-war movements—have we been able to rattle the political chessboard where government bodies and corporations move their pieces. The individual players at the board change, but the institutional game does not. Some of those players are better or worse than others—but our salvation does not rest in a shift of personnel among the oligarchy's leading servants. Our best possibilities can be nurtured as we activate ourselves to change the groundrules and insist that people are not pawns. Our true hope is in *democracy,* yet to be created.

III

"False hope is better than no hope."

Those words, spoken with evident irritation, came from an experienced activist when I mentioned the title of this book. The Clinton presidency was in its eighth month.

Since then the statement has returned to my mind many times. *False hope is better than no hope.* An expression of cynicism? Despair? Fear? Desire for comforts of deception? Labels don't seem very helpful. What kept striking me was the underlying mood of a tacit deal—psychological as much as political—as if to make peace with President Clinton and what he represents. A white flag waved at wealth and misery. A way to pretend that slight breezes of reform are strong winds of change.

False hope. No hope. Two ways of surrendering to dominant power. Those are not our only options.

Our authentic hope can be found elsewhere. Regardless of how we might prefer to describe the

choices—political, spiritual, ethical, moral, existen-
tial—they loom in front of us every day. How will we
respond to human imperatives? Will we endeavor to
speak clearly? Will we contribute to a culture of resistance and find sustenance from it? Will we affirm the
desperate need for radical change and struggle for it?

"If there is no struggle there is no progress,"
Frederick Douglass wrote in 1849. "Those who pro-
fess to favor freedom and yet deprecate agitation,"
he added, "want crops without plowing up the
ground. They want rain without thunder and lightning. They want the ocean without the awful roar of
its many waters." Douglass was writing to a white
abolitionist in the middle of the 19th century, but
his words are as current as each moment in the last
few years of the 20th century: "The struggle may be
a moral one; or it may be a physical one; or it may
be both moral and physical, but it must be a struggle. Power concedes nothing without a demand. It
never did and it never will."

The belief that power runs primarily through
the ballot box is a delusion. Consider the painful
realities of rural areas in the Deep South: As valiant
and pivotal as the battles for voting-rights were
three decades ago, today the shell of electoral
democracy is hollow next to the power of predatory
economics. The rule of capital is overpowering.
Dollars exercise the most powerful franchise. In
Mississippi, after four years as Jonestown's mayor,
Bobbie Walker said in 1993: "You're in charge, but
how much can you do? We have 1,476 people, but
we may have 100 who actually work. Almost all the
stores have closed. The town is basically broke.
People expect miracles because there are black peo-

ple in office, but this town is so strapped, and the tax base is so small, you can barely stay afloat."

What voting can't accomplish, community organizing and clarity in public debate and forthright action might. *Power concedes nothing without a demand. It never did and it never will.* The power overwhelming us, more than ever in the Clinton era, is the power of big corporations. With their wheels of fortune spinning, the solutions must come, first and foremost, from us.

IV

Realism about the Clinton presidency shouldn't be confused with cynicism or passivity. On the contrary: By resolving to fight for what we believe in, we revitalize idealism and activism. By refusing to defer to Clintonism, we can engage in substantive political encounters instead of retreating from them.

The kind of coalition-building that put Harold Washington in the mayor's office in Chicago a decade ago—overcoming the opposition of national party liberals like Edward Kennedy and Walter Mondale in the process—is a model that we should never forget. A well-organized coalition made it possible for Mayor Washington to push against timeworn corruption and privilege in Chicago. The multiracial movement behind him showed that big-city politics need not be dominated by the corporate flackery that so often kept black faces in high places from Atlanta to Detroit to Los Angeles during the 1980s.

Nor should we cede any ground to the liberal-conservative "spectrum" in elections for state and federal offices. A number of progressives in Congress today—like the independent socialist

Representative Bernie Sanders of Vermont and Senator Carol Moseley-Braun of Illinois—owe their successes to meticulous political organizing over a period of many years.

Yet even the most laudable politicians are hardly flawless, and would not be able to bring about basic change even if they were "perfect." We need to insist on holding all politicians accountable, while realizing the limitations of electoral avenues that do not reach the centers of economic power. Meanwhile, necessity calls for fighting a profusion of virulent ballot measures that are often anti-gay, anti-poor or anti-immigrant. On a more upbeat note, community groups have been exploring ways to put positive initiatives in front of voters.

But our greatest assets do not revolve around what happens on election day. Our strengths are rooted in the potential to be everything that politicians rarely are—direct, truthful, and eager to contest the arrogance of entrenched power with collective social action.

In 1993, thousands of activists concerned about health care didn't wait—they intensified efforts to create a Canadian-style, single-payer nationwide system in the United States. From the outset, they refused to go along with Bill and Hillary and the behind-closed-doors Jackson Hole Group— the elite panel fine-tuning a "managed competition" scenario that could have been titled the "Insurance Industry Preservation Act." (Huge insurance companies were central to drawing up the "managed competition" plan; insurance firms were important early contributors to Clinton's presidential campaign, and donated $850,000 to the Democratic Party in 1992.)

Coalitions including health care workers, consumer rights groups and labor unions helped to force debate about single-payer options onto the national political agenda—despite the dismissive attitudes of news media and mainstream politicians. With the Clinton administration insisting that insurance companies remain at the center of the U.S. medical system, many progressives kept fighting for truly universal and democratic health care.

No major victories are assured. The easy triumphs are the empty ones. Yet, from local neighborhoods to national politics to global forums, people are organizing to fulfill the imperatives of justice. However much it has been degraded and sentimentalized, the human spirit endures—capable of wondrous achievements in the past, and in the future. *Si se puede.* Yes it can be done.

V

Why is it so important to dispel false hopes? Clear political analysis hardly guarantees progressive social change, but without such analysis we won't get very far. As Noam Chomsky has commented, "It's very hard to get to the point where you can even discuss alternatives until you first peel away layer after layer of myth and illusion."

The great social transformations have come from people working together, sharing ideas—sometimes painfully—and finding ways to evolve from powerlessness to action; organizing independent movements, not looking for an official or a hero or a leader to do it for us; seeing that we can enliven ourselves and each other—that we can create history (not consume it like Wonder Bread). The breakthroughs can happen at meetings and community gatherings, during educational campaigns and marches and teach-ins and sit-ins and strikes and boycotts, via long-term projects with plenty of difficulties along the way, when people directly confront obstacles, when human energies climb out of the undertows of despair and turn instead into forward motion, moving the turbines of our possibilities.

I've seen it happen: on picket lines in front of segregated housing; as we walked through the sky-scrapered canyons of New York City in numbers exceeding 100,000 for the first time, to voice anguish and rage at the war on Vietnam; when we picketed supermarkets for selling scab lettuce; when we marched in a counter-inaugural procession along Pennsylvania Avenue; as we met and planned and protested and went to jail, going from draft board office to corporate headquarters to federal building; when we rallied in support of Native American rights as the modern siege of Wounded Knee continued; as we sat in front of nuclear power plant gates and filled jails in one county after another; as we stood on drawbridges and forced military ships to delay their arrivals in port; as we sat in front of a white train carrying nuclear warheads and stopped the death cargo motionless in its tracks for hours; as we canvassed and leafleted and marched to stop the slaughter in Central America, and the brutality of apartheid in South Africa; as we went to the Nevada Test Site, again and again, to end the explosions of nuclear bombs underneath the desert; as we demonstrated to stop violence against people of color; as we demanded jobs and justice and health care for all...

"The Fierce Urgency of *Now*"

Being part of such events has made me feel joy and solidarity that can never expire. We've made mistakes; we've learned some lessons much later than we might have. But marvelous potential has sometimes become reality. The best occurrences took place not by magic or by the leadership of any few geniuses; people did not wait for any president or other politician to say yes or no, they moved with all their doubts and fears and uncertainties to become more alive, and to create a better future.

Maybe back in the 1960s many people came to expect swift results—and then overreacted to disappointments, coming to settle for too little. But in the 1990s, thousands of organizations and millions of lives can trace their vitality to the cultural and political upsurges of the late '60s. Enduring legacies include networks of individuals and activist groups in every area of the United States. Our potential is enormous.

But we've got to be realistic about the Clinton political formulas: free immunization for poor children, and some kind of "managed competition," but no single-payer national health care system; Head Start funding but no commitment for decent housing or quality education or job opportunities for millions of impoverished children; lip-service for nature's wonders like old-growth forests and wetlands, but federal policies that will ravage more of them... We must avoid being trapped by ways that mass media and Democratic Party "pragmatists" frame issues. Unless we can build major counterpressure, President Clinton will continue to see wooing the center and center-right as his primary political goal. It's crucial that we shift the political debate of the country—not by pinning hopes on Clinton but, instead, by fighting for the changes we believe in. As a supporter of corporate power, Bill Clinton is doing his job. As opponents of that power, how well are we doing ours?

A movement challenging the power of corporations could include constituencies that are strongly anti-racist, feminist, environmentalist, pro-gay-rights, anti-militarist, pro-labor, anti-poverty, pro-full-employment, pro-consumer, and in favor of single-payer health care. The greatest taboos in mainstream politics and mass media are the most powerful keynotes for a grassroots political theme: analyzing corporate power and mobilizing opposition to it.

When AIDS activists adopted the slogan SILENCE = DEATH, they weren't engaging in hyperbole; inaction takes a cumulative toll, paid with lives. Meanwhile, ACTION = LIFE. If we speak up, if we organize more effectively, a lot could change. At home. At work. In public discourse. And in the political world, where power-brokers strain to prevent our awakening.

False hope encourages passivity and unending patience, as precious opportunities slip away. On the final page of his last book, Martin Luther King reminded us: "In this unfolding conundrum of life and history there is such a thing as being too late."

Near the end of a long ordeal in the labyrinths of the system—in response to the question "How am I being deluded?"—Franz Kafka provided a parable:

> In the writings which preface the Law that particular delusion is described thus: before the Law stands a doorkeeper. To this doorkeeper there comes a man from the country who begs

for admittance to the Law. But the doorkeeper says that he cannot admit the man at the moment. The man, on reflection, asks if he will be allowed, then, to enter later. "It is possible," answers the doorkeeper, "but not at this moment." Since the door leading into the Law stands open as usual and the doorkeeper steps to one side, the man bends down to peer through the entrance. When the doorkeeper sees that, he laughs and says: "If you are so strongly tempted, try to get in without my permission. But note that I am powerful. And I am only the lowest doorkeeper. From hall to hall, keepers stand at every door, one more powerful than the other. And the sight of the third man is already more than even I can stand." These are difficulties which the man from the country has not expected to meet, the Law, he thinks, should be accessible to every man and at all times, but when he looks more closely at the doorkeeper in his furred robe, with his huge, pointed nose and long, thin, Tartar beard, he decides that he had better wait until he gets permission to enter. The doorkeeper gives him a stool and lets him sit down at the side of the door. There he sits waiting for days and years. He makes many attempts to be allowed in and wearies the doorkeeper with his importunity. The doorkeeper often engages him in brief conversation, asking him about his home and about other matters, but the questions are put quite impersonally, as great men put questions, and always conclude with the statement that the man cannot be allowed to enter yet. The man, who has equipped himself with many things for his journey, parts with all he has, however valuable, in the hope of bribing the doorkeeper. The doorkeeper accepts it all, say-

193

ing, however, as he takes each gift: "I take this only to keep you from feeling that you have left something undone." During all these long years the man watches the doorkeeper almost incessantly. He forgets about the other doorkeepers, and this one seems to him the only barrier between himself and the Law. In the first years he curses his evil fate aloud; later, as he grows old, he only mutters to himself. He grows childish, and since in his prolonged study of the doorkeeper he has learned to know even the fleas in his fur collar, he begs the very fleas to help him and to persuade the doorkeeper to change his mind. Finally his eyes grow dim and he does not know whether the world is really darkening around him or whether his eyes are only deceiving him. But in the darkness he can now perceive a radiance that streams inextinguishably from the door of the Law. Now his life is drawing to a close. Before he dies, all that he has experienced during the whole time of his sojourn condenses in his mind into one question, which he has never yet put to the doorkeeper. He beckons the doorkeeper, since he can no longer raise his stiffening body. The doorkeeper has to bend far down to hear him, for the difference in size between them has increased very much to the man's disadvantage. "What do you want to know now?" asks the doorkeeper, "you are insatiable." "Everyone strives to attain the Law," answers the man, "how does it come about, then, that in all these years no one has come seeking admittance but me?" The doorkeeper perceives that the man is nearing his end and his hearing is failing, so he bellows in his ear: "No one but you could gain admittance through this door, since this door was intended for you. I am now going to shut it."

Notes

Chapter One:
And the Invisible Hand Plays On

25 Riddle: "What do Washington's politicians and pro wrestlers have in common?... They're mostly overweight white guys pretending to hurt each other."

25 Thomas L. Friedman, *New York Times*, June 20, 1993.

26 "this image of the mighty...," Mark Crispin Miller, *Boxed In: The Culture of TV*, p. 87.

27 The examples of corporate donors to the Democratic Leadership Council are from William Greider, *Who Will Tell the People*, p. 263.

27 "Fiscal conservatism and social liberalism...," Hobart Rowen, *Washington Post*, November 8, 1992.

27 Clinton's position on abortion has been one of his important lures for younger voters. As E.J. Dionne Jr. notes in *Why Americans Hate Politics* (p. 342), "the polls suggest that younger women are far more pro-choice than the rest of the female population."

28 Clinton won the presidency with a lot of help from gay men and lesbians, receiving "nearly 75 percent" of their votes (*Newsweek*, May 3, 1993) in contrast to about half for Dukakis four years earlier.

28 Stuart Eizenstat quoted in *Washington Post*, November 6, 1992. Eizenstat works as a lawyer advocating for corporations.

28 "signals to the American people...," Clinton quoted

195

in *Boston Globe,* May 30, 1993.

29   "shift to the right...," *Newsweek,* June 14, 1993.

29   The *New York Times* editorial that angered Mark Shields was titled "A History of Gergenism." It appeared on June 2, 1993.

29   Mark Shields, "The David Gergen I Know," *Washington Post,* June 5, 1993.

29   Gergen's criticism of the Clinton administration for "emphasizing tax increases over spending cuts" appeared in his *U.S. News & World Report* column (May 10, 1993). Gergen lamented that Clinton's initial performance as president was disappointing: "After running the best Democratic campaign of modern times, his team has also made a surprising number of mistakes in the White House: lurching to the left too often, emphasizing tax increases over spending cuts, treating adversaries with arrogant disdain and gradually losing a central thrust to its leadership.... If [Clinton] doesn't have all the right answers, we should stop jeering, get off the sidelines and help him find them. For the next 1,300 days, he is the only president we have."

29   As a magazine columnist and TV pundit, David Gergen was part of the media chorus bemoaning President Clinton's initial (and imaginary) "lurch to the left." Even after Gergen was hired as the White House's new media honcho, *Time* (June 7, 1993) sniffed: "Gergen says he is 'convinced' Clinton wants to 'run a bipartisan government.' But other than Gergen's appointment itself, there has been scant evidence of any commitment to the middle." Later that month, the quintessential judge of political balance William Safire wrote a *New York Times* column (June 21) explaining: "The First Clinton Administration, marked by the surprise leftward

lurch, is presumably over; the Second Clinton Administration, or S.C.A., is upon us; centrism is in the saddle..."

29   All the talk about a "lurch to the left" in the first few months of the Clinton administration appealed to anti-left media, as well as to leftists eager to believe that they indeed had a friend in the White House at last. One of the few astute responses in mass media came from the only honest-to-goodness leftist with a regular column in a national newsweekly, Barbara Ehrenreich—who pointed out in *Time* (June 21, 1993) that Clinton's already-fabled lurch to the left was "a neat parable, but it never happened." She added: "The lurch to the left is like the 'stab in the back' invented by right-wing Germans after World War One: an instant myth designed to discredit all one's political enemies in one fell swoop. Ask anyone who hangs out in left field—columnists for the *Nation,* for instance, or resident thinkers at Washington's Institute for Policy Studies—and they'll tell you there hasn't been any lurching in their direction. A few tentative little steps perhaps—abolition of the 'gag rule' on abortions, the signing of the 'motor voter' and family-leave bills, some vague reformist intentions here and there—followed by an inexorable stagger to the right.... Maybe it's been so long that we've forgotten what 'left' is and how to tell it from right. At the simplest, most ecumenical level, to be on the left means to take the side of the underdog, whoever that may be: the meek, the poor and, generally speaking, the 'least among us,' as a well-known representative of the left position put it a couple of millenniums ago. Thus it is not leftish to have a $200 haircut while planes full of $20 haircut people circle overhead; nor would a leftist contemplate selling the president's favors at $15,000 a plate

fund raisers. Such behaviors belong way over on the right, along with supply-side economics, capital-gains tax reductions and other efforts to pamper the pâté-eating classes.... [Clinton] *felt* for the underdog, as he never tired of telling us, but whenever the overdogs began to howl, he obediently rushed back toward the right.... [Clinton's economic program] maintains military spending at cold-war levels, thus foreclosing any serious new spending on domestic programs.... It's an attempt, in other words, to mix LBJ, Reagan and Ross Perot— which is why it comes out as such a flavorless gruel."

30   "reportedly secured a promise...," *Newsweek,* July 12, 1993.

30   Gergen was hardly secretive about his mission. As soon as President Clinton announced the hiring, Gergen went on CNN to declare: "I think the president wants to be more centrist." (*Time,* June 7, 1993.) And Gergen told the *Boston Globe* that the night before accepting the job he had a long talk with Clinton about "what was going on in his presidency, where he was philosophically, where he thought he was going." Gergen added: "I didn't want to come in unless I thought I could make a difference. If I thought he was careening down a liberal path, I'd have been so uncomfortable with that I couldn't have done it." But, as the *Boston Globe* (May 30, 1993) reported, "Clinton's responses on the fundamental questions of political philosophy, handling of the press and partisanship were 'music to my ears,' Gergen said."

30   For a discussion of "the takeover of the Democratic Party" in 1992, see *Adventures in Medialand: Behind the News, Beyond the Pundits* (Common Courage Press, 1993), by Jeff Cohen and Norman

Solomon, pp. 36-40.

30   The Democratic National Committee's daily behind-
the-scenes memo with talking points (headed "The
Morning Briefing" and faxed to press secretaries for
Democrats on Capitol Hill) was mostly devoted to a
section titled "The President's Plan—Good For
Business" on the first Friday of June 1993:
"Business leaders throughout the country have ral-
lied behind the President's economic plan. They
know that the President's plan makes the tough
choices we need to reduce the deficit and restore
economic growth to the country. The following is a
list of some of the businesses that have voiced their
support for the President's economic plan: Aflac
Incorporated, Ameritech Corp., Associated
Financial Corp., Beneficial Corp., Colgate-Palmolive
Corp., Dow Corning Corp., Emerson Electric Co.,
GenCorp Inc., General Mills Inc., General Signals
Corp., Honeywell Inc., IBM, Kellog Company, 3M,
Mars Inc., Owens-Corning Fiberglass Corp., PLY
GEM Industries Inc., The Procter & Gamble
Company, The Quaker Oats Company, Sara Lee
Corp., Southern California Edison Co., Southland
Corp., Tektronix Inc., Time Warner Inc., The Walt
Disney Company, Allied Signal Inc., Anheuser-
Busch Companies Inc., Avon Products Inc., B.P.
America, Delta Air Lines Inc., Electronic Data
Systems, The GAP Inc., General Electric Company,
General Motors Corp., Hallmark Cards Inc.,
Hughes Aircraft Company, Jim Walker Corp., Levi
Strauss & Co., Marriott Corp., Mercantile Stores
Co. Inc., Philip Morris Companies Inc., Premark
International Inc., Puget Power Corp., Ryder
System Inc., Service Merchandise Co. Inc.,
Southern California Gas Co., Southwest Airlines
Company, Tenneco Inc., Valero Energy Corp.,
Westinghouse Electric Corp."

Chapter Two:
'60s Memories, '90s Distress

31   Bill Clinton's overall margin of 5 percent over Bush in the 1992 popular vote was as high as it was because Clinton did well among baby boomers and even better among younger voters. Exit polling showed Clinton with a 6 percent advantage in the populous 30-to-44 age range, the same 6 percent lead among 25-to-29 years olds, and a 16 percent edge among voters 18-to-24 (*Time* Magazine, November 16, 1992). "One reason was Clinton's limber courtship of the young in show-biz terms— playing his sax on the Arsenio Hall show, for instance, and featuring rock music at his rallies," *Time* commented. "But recent high school and college graduates facing a bleak employment market had more substantive reasons for abandoning the G.O.P." The contrast with Michael Dukakis's dismal 1988 showing among middle-aged and younger voters was striking: Dukakis lost to Bush by 9 percent in the 30-to-44 age range; by 15 percent among ages 25-to-29; and by 5 percent among 18-to-24 voters.

32   Thirty years ago, Herbert Marcuse saw a centralized high-tech threat looming large on the horizon. "By virtue of the way it has organized its technological base, contemporary industrial society tends to be totalitarian," he wrote. "For 'totalitarian' is not only a terroristic political coordination of society, but also a non-terroristic economic-technical coordination which operates through the manipulation of needs by vested interests. It thus precludes the emergence of an effective opposition against the whole." Yet it is just such opposition that is needed in the mid-1990s.

32   "President Clinton was elected on a platform of cre-

ating high-tech, high-wage jobs," Patrick J. Lucey reminded *New York Times* readers in an op-ed piece published July 13, 1993. Lucey, a former U.S. ambassador to Mexico, was arguing in favor of the North American Free Trade Agreement.

32 In November 1992, Clinton received 82 percent of the black vote—"the lowest percentage garnered by a Democratic presidential candidate since 1960," according to the head of the Council of 100, a group of black Republicans (Milton Bins, letter, *New York Times,* July 13, 1993).

34 "The country is not clamoring...," Christopher Matthews on "Face the Nation," CBS, April 19, 1993.

34 For a description of media spin on urban conditions, see "Business as Usual After L.A. Verdict" in FAIR's magazine *Extra!,* July/August 1993. (An *Extra!* subscription, $30 per year, is available by calling 1-800-847-3993 or by mail: FAIR/*Extra!,* Subscription Service, P.O. Box 911, Dept. V3JE, Pearl River, NY 10965.)

36 The *New England Journal of Medicine* (September 24, 1992) published a study which concluded that "the Gulf War and trade sanctions caused a three-fold increase in mortality among Iraqi children under 5 years of age. We estimate that an excess of more than 46,900 children died between January and August 1991." Two years after the war, available figures indicated that about 100,000 Iraqis under age 5 had died as a result of the war and the embargo spearheaded by the U.S. government. Such reports drew only fleeting media coverage in the United States. Meanwhile, there was no shortage of heart-wrenching journalism about the brutal suppression of Kurds by the Baghdad government. The *New York Times Magazine,* for example, fea-

tured the subject in its first cover story of 1993, "Iraq Accused: A Case of Genocide."

36   "We should all be justly proud of our magnificent victory in the Gulf," Clinton said in his keynote address to the Democratic Leadership Council's national convention in Cleveland on May 6, 1991. It was the kind of statement Clinton liked to repeat that spring, contrasting Gulf War glories with domestic difficulties, as when he told a Louisiana audience on May 18: "My message today is that while we're all very proud of our military victory in the Persian Gulf, we all know that all is not well in America."

36   "As the nation's first baby-boomer president, Clinton will bring to the Oval Office a fresh mental map of generational impressions," reported *Time* (November 16, 1992). "Gone are the Andrews Sisters, Kilroy and the Berlin blockade. In their place come 'Father Knows Best,' Elvis, 1960s folk music (Chelsea Clinton was named after the Joni Mitchell song 'Chelsea Morning'), Vietnam protests, the 1972 George McGovern crusade and Watergate."

36   "But if Clinton becomes...," Editor's Note, *Mother Jones,* July/August 1993.

37   The notion of Bill Clinton embodying the baby-boom generation has been a media staple. For instance, when he became the Democratic presidential nominee, a four-page magazine spread about his life (*Newsweek,* July 20, 1992) carried the headline, "SIXTIES Coming of Age."

38   Eager for a sense of meaning and stability, a startling number of young adults in the 1970s grabbed onto guide-rails provided by a panoply of gurus, maharishis, preachers, fee-charging visionaries and

other self-proclaimed experts on human existence. Much was promised, but much less delivered. That a person couldn't very well plug into enlightenment, like an appliance into a wall socket, should have been more obvious than it was. Following the right spiritual teacher was no more a solution than ingesting the right drugs. Brought up in a materialistic culture and an evermore service-oriented economy, maybe we found it "natural" to look for specific substances or entrepreneurs to give us what we really needed. Sometimes we figured that they could point us in the best direction for a lifelong journey—or even take us on it. But with our own inner lives so mystified, it was doubtful that external stimuli would illuminate very much for us.

Chapter Three:
JFK, Clinton and the Politics of Myth

39   *Time* (July 27, 1992) singled out the movie about Clinton as one of "three carefully plotted moves" that produced "Clinton's success" at the Democratic National Convention. "The fourteen-minute biographical film that preceded Clinton's acceptance speech," the magazine reported, "began the arduous task of creating empathy for a candidate carrying enough political baggage to fill a container ship."

39   In August 1993, when President Clinton took his first extended holiday since moving into the White House, he chose to vacation at Martha's Vineyard— along the stretch of coastline made famous by John Kennedy. The news media dutifully administered another heavy dose of Camelot nostalgia to Clinton's presidential image. Typical was a *New York Times* article (August 25) headlined "Clinton and Kennedys: In 30 Years, a Full Circle." It was

manifest torch-passing all over again, beginning with the article's lead: "Thirty years ago, Bill Clinton the boy stood staring at John F. Kennedy, his hero, in the White House Rose Garden. Today, Jacqueline Kennedy Onassis and other members of the family welcomed Bill Clinton the president to the seas off the Massachusetts coast that his murdered predecessor loved so well." The *Times* noted that Clinton "has devoted much of his political career to casting himself as a Southern apostle of John F. Kennedy.... Unlike most recent presidents, Mr. Clinton has done much to honor and emulate President Kennedy. On the day before he was sworn into office in January, he traveled to Arlington National Cemetery to visit the graves of John and Robert F. Kennedy, and with members of the Kennedy family put white roses there.... As he has consciously tried to emulate the vigor of President Kennedy, Mr. Clinton has been aided by youth. Mr. Clinton was forty-six when he was inaugurated; Mr. Kennedy was forty-three. Mr. Clinton has also recalled on multiple occasions how he was moved to choose a career in public service after he met Mr. Kennedy in a Rose Garden ceremony as a delegate to Boys' Nation in 1963. His mother has said that he decided he would be president that day."

41 I can remember seeing, for many years after the assassination, dusty plates with President Kennedy's face on them, displayed in storefront windows near Pennsylvania Avenue. The stores themselves, located between the White House and Capitol, seemed to me to have been frozen in time, like the room where Miss Havisham's wedding cake had turned to ghastly cobwebs in *Great Expectations*. "From that room...the daylight was completely excluded," Dickens wrote, "and it had

an airless smell that was oppressive. A fire had been lately kindled in the damp old-fashioned grate, and it was more disposed to go out than to burn up, and the reluctant smoke which hung in the room seemed colder than the clearer air—like our own marsh mist. Certain wintry branches of candles on the high chimney-piece faintly lighted the chamber, or, it would be more expressive to say, faintly troubled its darkness. It was spacious, and I dare say had once been handsome, but every discernible thing in it was covered with dust and mould, and dropping to pieces. The most prominent object was a long table with a table-cloth spread on it, as if a feast had been in preparation when the house and the clocks all stopped together."

42   For an analysis of media attacks on Oliver Stone's movie "JFK," see *Adventures in Medialand,* pp. 214-18.

42   By the way, in the "JFK" film, the tears welling in Kevin Costner's eyes came from an actor who in real life has such unprogressive politics that he contributed thousands of dollars to the campaign coffers of hard-right Republican Senator Phil Gramm of Texas. In 1990, Costner gave $4,000 for Gramm's re-election effort. (*Texas Observer,* May 31, 1991.) A photo of the pair later graced a "Gramm in '96" brochure.

42   "When John F. Kennedy took office, he launched the Alliance for Progress, a program of help for Latin America, emphasizing social reform to better the lives of people," Howard Zinn notes in *A People's History of the United States* (p. 430). "But it turned out to be mostly military aid to keep in power right-wing dictatorships and enable them to stave off revolutions."

42　For some particulars on John Kennedy's presidential policies, see *A People's History of the United States*, pp. 428-29, 432, 434, 515-16, 548. Details about grim aspects of President Kennedy's record can be found in *Rethinking Camelot* by Noam Chomsky.

43　Although Jerry Brown denounced corporate power while running for president in 1992, his campaign's "Take Back America" slogan echoed the myth that the people of the United States had once controlled the country.

44　"The great leaders are...," Frank Greer, quoted in *Newsweek*, March 30, 1992.

44　"THE TORCH PASSES...," *Newsweek*, November/December 1992 special issue.

45　"Now the torch is being...," *Time*, November 16, 1992.

45　"For years, Americans have been...," *Time*, January 4, 1993. Accompanied by the much-enlarged image of President Kennedy from the photo snapped at the moment his path crossed with Bill Clinton's, the article went on to note: "As a sixteen-year-old member of Boy's Nation, Clinton stood in the Rose Garden of the White House in 1963 and shook hands with John Kennedy—an instant of symbolic torch passing that had a powerful effect upon the ambitious boy from Hope, Arkansas."

45　With Bill Clinton as designated driver, the Democratic Party veered rightward in 1992 while he tossed out populist rhetoric now and again to cover tracks. Midway through the year, Barbara Ehrenreich commented that "even Clinton, avatar of the Democratic Leadership Council's strategy of mimicking the Republican Party, went around indignantly reciting the fact that the very rich, referring to the top 1 percent in terms of income, had hogged 60 percent of the economic growth in the last dozen years." (*Mother Jones,* July/August 1992.)

46   "Our presidents at their inaugurals...," I.F. Stone, *Polemics and Prophecies: 1967-1970* (Vintage Books edition), p. 120.

47   "I realize that it will always...," John F. Kennedy, *The Strategy of Peace,* p. 172. Kennedy was speaking to a dinner audience in Puerto Rico.

47   For an account of President-elect Kennedy's meeting with Robert A. Lovett, see David Halberstam's book *The Best and the Brightest,* pp. 3-10. Wrote Halberstam: "That cold December day Kennedy was lunching with a man who not only symbolized a group, the Establishment, and was a power broker who carried the proxies for the great law firms and financial institutions, but was also tied to a great and seemingly awesome era. If Kennedy, as he always did in that period, complained that he knew no experts, that was no problem; the Establishment had long lists and it would be delighted to co-operate with this young President, help him along. It was of course above politics. It feared the right...and it feared the left; it held what was proclaimed to be the center." (*The Best and the Brightest,* p. 8.)

47   Three decades after Defense Secretary Robert McNamara was gearing up to deploy more U.S. troops to Vietnam, Bill Clinton chose to stay at McNamara's home on Oyster Bay in Massachusetts during his ten-day presidential vacation in late August 1993.

48   "a national security team...," Leslie Gelb, *New York Times,* November 5, 1992.

48   "The most consistent thing...," Christopher
      Hitchens, the *Nation*, July 5, 1993.

48   "President-elect Bill Clinton intends to make good
      on his promise to end the military's ban on gays
      soon after the Inauguration—at least in some
      form," reported a brief item in *Newsweek*
      (December 14, 1992). The magazine quoted "a top
      adviser" as saying: "He's not going to waffle..."

49   "no new substantive or procedural...," Defense
      Department's general counsel Jamie S. Gorelick
      quoted in *San Francisco Chronicle*, July 22, 1993.

49   "It sends a very strong...," Randy Shilts quoted in
      New York Times, July 21, 1993.

49   "acceded, without a fight...," Thomas Stoddard
      quoted in *New York Times*, July 20, 1993.

49   "No matter how they try...," David Mixner quoted in
      New York Times, July 18, 1993.

49   Even when President Clinton claimed he was going
      to lift the ban on openly gay people in the military,
      some dubious dynamics were at work. "Bill Clinton
      was acting on a campaign promise made to the gay
      community in general, but a promise really made to
      those wealthy, white gay men who raised millions
      of dollars for his election campaign," a longtime
      activist in the lesbian/gay movement, Leslie Cagan,
      has pointed out. "It is some of these same people
      who poured at least one and a half million dollars
      into the newly-created Campaign for Military
      Service, a D.C.-based effort formed to secure the
      lifting of the ban. As one of the best-funded organi-
      zations in the lesbian/gay community it is no won-
      der they are able to set the terms of the debate. It is
      unfortunate that the terms they are setting are so
      mainstream, so unquestioning and accepting of the
      institution. The only question raised is the right of

lesbians and gay men to serve in the military. No questions about the role of the military, or what drives most people to sign up these days, or how the military interfaces with other structures of domination and control, internationally and right here at home." (*Independent Political Action Bulletin,* Summer 1993; available from IPAB, P.O. Box 170610, Brooklyn, NY 11217.)

49 David Mixner "raised roughly $1 million for Bill Clinton in 1992," according to *Newsweek.* To his credit, Mixner—widely reported to be a good friend of Clinton's—was among dozens of gay-rights activists arrested for civil disobedience in front of the White House on July 30, 1993, after Clinton broke his promise to order an end to anti-gay discrimination in the U.S. military.

49 "Bill Clinton is very good on lesbian and gay issues," Roberta Achtenberg told radio listeners on the last day of the 1992 Democratic Convention. She went on: "I like Bill Clinton. I know him. I think he's got a heart and a soul still, despite the lofty heights to which he has ascended. I think he's a good guy with decent instincts. He's very smart and he's educatable. I like him very much personally. He's a friend. I've tried to influence him and will continue, and on lesbian and gay rights he has promised to produce certain things and I want to hold him to those promises.... I think that he has some heart and soul left, some center in his life. And quite frankly the rest is strategy and politics and wanting to make him beholden to this community and going out and delivering money and votes and having him write it down on paper and hope that some of the promises will be kept." (Achtenberg was interviewed live on the "Convention Watch" national radio broadcast, at the studios of WBAI, on July 16, 1992.) A member

of the San Francisco board of supervisors, Achtenberg had made an early endorsement of Clinton's presidential candidacy. In 1993 she became the highest-ranking openly gay person in the federal executive branch, when the Senate confirmed her nomination by President Clinton to become the assistant secretary for fair housing and equal opportunity at the U.S. Department of Housing and Urban Development.

50   "the stale orthodoxies of...," Bill Clinton, May 6, 1991.

51   Speaking on the CBS television program "Face the Nation" the weekend before the 1988 Democratic Convention began, host Lesley Stahl recited Michael Dukakis's preferences and added: "This is supposed to be his convention." On NBC, Tom Brokaw suggested that Jesse Jackson might be "on an ego trip." A few days earlier, in the *Washington Post* (July 14, 1988), savant David Broder wrote that Dukakis "showed he understands that it is more important to collect electoral votes than to court or console individual constituencies." By the time the gavel fell in Atlanta, "constituencies" sounded like code for uppity niggers, queers, bitches, riffraff. On the front page of Sunday's *Los Angeles Times* (July 17, 1988) was the flat-out journalistic statement, neither quoted nor attributed, that "the Rev. Jesse Jackson sows frustration and anxiety throughout the Democratic Party." Affluent white America was master of the game, expert at nothing if not definitions and the means to purvey them.

52   For details and analysis of how the press has treated Jackson's efforts in relation to the national Democratic Party, see *Unreliable Sources: A Guide to Detecting Bias in News Media* by Martin A. Lee

Notes to pages 54-60

and Norman Solomon, pp. 156-58; and *Adventures in Medialand*, pp. 129-32.

54 Clinton described E.J. Dionne Jr. as a "very gifted political writer" in a speech to the annual state convention of the Wisconsin Democratic Party in Milwaukee on June 15, 1991.

54 "liberalism and conservatism are framing...," E.J. Dionne, *Why Americans Hate Politics*, p. 11.

55 "broad middle class," Dionne, p. 27.

55 "America's restive middle class," Dionne, p. 344.

55 "the restive majority...," Dionne, p. 345.

55 "a new politics of the middle class...," Dionne, p. 326.

55 "new political center," Dionne, p. 27.

55 "Eighties Right" and "Sixties Left," Dionne, p. 330.

55 "voters increasingly look for...," Dionne, p. 345.

57 "If you want to know...," Dionne, p. 353. The italics in this quotation are Dionne's.

58 "After years of political game-playing...," Dionne, p. 9.

58 The column by Arthur Schlesinger Jr. referring to slaves as "involuntary immigrants" appeared in the *Wall Street Journal* on June 25, 1991.

58 "In our efforts to find...," Dionne, p. 355.

59 Alice's dialectical discussion with Humpty Dumpty occurred in Lewis Carroll's *Through the Looking-Glass.*

59 "The political needs of society...," Herbert Marcuse, *One-Dimensional Man*, pp. xli-xlii.

60 Roland Barthes quoted in Herbert Marcuse, *One-*

211

Dimensional Man, p. 101.

60   "freedom of the press...," A.J. Liebling, *The Press*, p. 32.

61   "an instrument of control...," Marcuse, *One-Dimensional Man*, p. 103.

61   "If the language of politics...," Marcuse, p. 103.

62   "We Americans like to think of ourselves as rootin' tootin' individualists," I.F. Stone wrote in 1952, yet we "read the same news-agency reports in the same kind of newspapers, take in the same ideas from the same big national magazines, and listen solemnly to the same platitudes from the two big— and very much the same—political parties." (*The Truman Era*, p. 217.)

Chapter Four:
Long Winding Road

63   Billy Gray quoted in *Favorite Families of TV* (pp. 50-52) by Christopher Paul Denis and Michael Denis.

64   James Baldwin raised questions about assumptions behind integration scenarios in *The Fire Next Time.*

67   Compare President Johnson's statement on April 10, 1965 ("We love peace. We hate war. But our course is charted always by the compass of honor.") with President Bush's on August 18, 1988: "And I hate war. Love peace. And we have peace. And I am not going to let anyone take it away from us."

70   James Baldwin, *No Name in the Street*, pp. 178, 183-84, 186-88. The book was published by The Dial Press in 1972.

77   Gore Vidal and William F. Buckley appeared on the

ABC television network as commentators during the '68 Democratic Convention. At one point Buckley burst out: "Now listen, you queer, stop calling me a crypto-Nazi or I'll sock you in the goddamn face and you'll stay plastered."

77   Danny Schechter, *Boston Phoenix,* September 5, 1972. His article also observed: "It seems clear that the networks have decided to diminish, if not reverse, their role as radical organizer. On the convention floor, Spiro's supporters were telling the nation that their Agnew's media criticisms had gotten results. They were right. And so was the television coverage of the spectacle. It only paid peripheral coverage to the protest scene. When the convention itself became too dull even for Walter, CBS shifted outside—but most frequently to a helicopter shot.... John Chancellor's confession of befuddlement at what was happening in the streets echoed the decision to keep it that way...." Any role that television may have played as "radical organizer" for the anti-war cause was inadvertent. During the years of U.S. military escalation, the TV networks were fully supportive of the war in Vietnam, and doggedly negative toward the anti-war movement; later on, after the U.S. establishment began to split over war policies, TV framed the issues in terms of whether the war was "winnable" rather than whether it was morally criminal. Radical critiques of the war as barbaric aggression by the U.S. government were never given much air time. For a definitive history of the media's role in covering the Vietnam War, see Daniel C. Hallin's book *Uncensored War.*

78   Writing in *Saturday Review* in November 1971, Peter Schrag commented a year before Nixon's re-election: "The American majority is against the war. To oppose it involves no risk: the only risk lies in

213

trying to stop it."

80 Jimmy Carter was too old to be in the baby-boom generation, but he created a small sensation by quoting Bob Dylan and associating himself with a few rock stars.

80 "the destruction was mutual," Jimmy Carter, March 24, 1977.

80 The eventual demise of the MX missile system was not for lack of President Carter's all-out support.

80 "The Carter administration initiated plans to sharply increase military expenditures and cut back social programs in 1978, and then exploited the subsequent Iran hostage crisis and Soviet invasion of Afghanistan to demonstrate the need" for a big boost in Pentagon spending, Noam Chomsky writes in *Turning the Tide* (p. 205).

81 The percentages for social-program growth rates during the Nixon, Ford and Carter administrations are cited in Noam Chomsky, *Turning the Tide,* p. 242.

81 "The Carter administration halted the creation...," Manning Marable, *Black American Politics,* p. 250.

81 For a discussion of how Reagan's military outlays and budget alterations picked up the thread of Carter's planning and projections, see Noam Chomsky, *Deterring Democracy,* p. 81 and p. 254.

81 "By 1977, Indonesia had actually...," Chomsky, *The Chomsky Reader,* p. 306.

82 For an account of President Carter's role in El Salvador, see Noam Chomsky, *Turning the Tide,* pp. 102-03. In the same book (p. 214), Chomsky comments: "In El Salvador...the Carter administration viewed the problem as a local one: its task was to conduct a massacre of sufficient scale to guarantee

the rule of the gangsters of its choice." Chomsky adds that the Reagan administration preferred to depict the Salvadoran conflict as part of a global struggle against an evil foe.

82   "Carter supported Somoza virtually...," Noam Chomsky, *Turning the Tide*, p. 128. Chomsky adds that "when all hope of maintaining Somoza was lost," President Carter saw to it that "the U.S. attempted to ensure that the National Guard would remain intact and the FSLN [Sandinistas] excluded from the government, a solution that the guerrillas accurately characterized as '*somocismo* without Somoza.'" For details about Carter's machinations in the midst of Nicaragua's revolution, see *Deterring Democracy*, p. 260 and pp. 312-13.

82   "U.S. military aid to the mass murderers...," Noam Chomsky, *Turning the Tide*, p. 156.

86   My inquiry about Mondale's positions on nuclear weapons was part of research for an op-ed article that appeared in the *Los Angeles Times* on December 28, 1982, under the headline "Nuclear-Freeze Proponents Must Fight Euromissiles."

86   "more fig leaf than litmus test..." quoted from my article in *San Jose Mercury News*, June 24, 1984. The article also said: "The former vice president accepts the assumptions that make nuclear weapons escalation inevitable. He is eager to sign on anti-nuclear voters who will not be reading the fine print of his positions.... When it comes to nuclear arsenals, the Democratic presidential standard-bearer will be offering scant substantive difference from the current Oval Office occupant.... Reagan has been depicted as the problem, despite the fact that he has maintained a trajectory set by the previous administration—increasing bellicosity toward the Soviets, and developing Carter-backed

nuclear weaponry such as the MX, Trident, cruise and Pershing 2 missiles."

88   "In the person of Walter Mondale..." quoted from my article written for Pacific News Service; it appeared in *Cleveland Plain Dealer,* November 18, 1984.

Chapter Five:
The Politics of News Media

91   "stopping short, as though by instinct...," George Orwell, *1984,* pp. 174-75.

91   In his afterword to *1984,* Erich Fromm emphasized "the point which is essential for the understanding of Orwell's book, namely that 'doublethink' is already with us, and not merely something which will happen in the future, and in dictatorships." (p. 265.)

92   "the special function of certain...," Orwell, *1984,* pp. 250-51.

93   "There is, of course, no...," Aldous Huxley, foreword published in 1946, *Brave New World,* p. xiv, p. xv.

94   For details on the swift consolidation of corporate media ownership in the United States, see *The Media Monopoly* (Fourth Edition) by Ben Bagdikian.

96   Walter Karp's assessment of U.S. journalism and "the fact of oligarchy" appeared in his article titled "All the Congressmen's Men" in *Harper's* Magazine, July 1989. "The news media in America do not tell the American people that a political whip hangs over their head," he wrote. "That is because a political whip hangs over their head."

97   "It is beyond doubt that...," Morton Mintz, *Nieman Reports,* Autumn 1991. "A built-in, chronic tilt

chills mainstream press coverage of grave, persisting, and pervasive abuses of corporate power," Mintz wrote. News media generally see themselves as watchdogs of government, but not of corporations. That, says Mintz, is a fatal journalistic flaw: "Underlying the pathetically inadequate coverage of life-threatening corporate misconduct is the everlasting embrace by the press of a truly absurd but wondrously convenient rationale for pro-corporate tilt: in an industrial society government constitutes the whole of governance."

97   I appeared with Bob Scheer on KFI Radio in Los Angeles, in December 1990. The program was hosted by Bill Handel, substituting for regular host Tom Leykis—a left-of-center personality later fired by KFI to make room for retiring Los Angeles police chief Daryl Gates to have a daily radio show. (The quotes from Scheer were transcribed from a tape of the program.)

98   "also owns other newspapers...," *The Media Monopoly*, pp. 39-40 (Second Edition). This superb book by Ben Bagdikian, a former editor at the *Washington Post*, was published in its fourth edition by Beacon Press in 1993.

98   In 1993 Scheer was writing often-laudable political pieces for various sections of the *San Francisco Examiner*.

99   "stopping short, as though by instinct...," Orwell, *1984*, p. 174.

99   "has to be conscious...," Orwell, *1984*, p. 176.

101 "First, it keeps us powerless...," Anne Wilson Schaef, *When Society Becomes an Addict*, pp. 65-66. The book was published in paperback by Harper San Francisco.

102 "The great triumphs of propaganda...," Aldous

Huxley, foreword, *Brave New World,* p. xv.

103   For details on the guest lists and sources used in daily news broadcasts on PBS ("The MacNeil/Lehrer NewsHour") and NPR ("All Things Considered" and "Morning Edition"), see *Adventures in Medialand,* p. 89 and pp. 231-33. Lengthy statistical analyses are available in studies released by FAIR, 130 W. 25th St., New York, NY 10001; (212) 633-6700.

103   After ten years as National Public Radio's president, Douglas Bennet left NPR to become an assistant secretary of state in May 1993. (By then the network was claiming ten million listeners each week for "All Things Considered" and "Morning Edition.") Succeeding Bennet was Delano Lewis, who moved to NPR from his post as president and CEO of the Chesapeake & Potomac Telephone Company.

105   *The Selling of the President, 1968* was authored by Joe McGinniss.

105   "What do we see...," Mark Crispin Miller, *Boxed In,* p. 157.

106   The revolving door between the war-makers and the war reporters kept spinning in 1993. In March, the man who had been the Bush administration's leading liar for the Pentagon, Pete Williams, started a new job—working as a national correspondent for NBC News in Washington. (For background on Williams' record of mendacities as a mouthpiece for the U.S. military during the invasion of Panama and the Gulf War, see *Adventures in Medialand,* pp. 182-84). In July the Pentagon announced that a former correspondent who'd covered the White House for ABC News, Kathleen deLaski, would become the first woman to serve as chief

spokesperson for the Defense Department.

106   The estimate of 200,000 Iraqi deaths during the six weeks of the Gulf War, coming from Pentagon officials a few weeks after the war ended, got very little media attention in the United States. For instance, *U.S. News & World Report* (April 1, 1991) devoted a total of two sentences to the estimate in the magazine's "Washington Whispers" section. The 200,000 figure was later cited by former Secretary of the Navy John Lehman when he spoke privately to other elite men at the annual Bohemian Grove conclave in summer 1991; Lehman titled his speech "Smart Weapons." (For details on Bohemian Grove, see *Adventures in Medialand,* pp. 2-4.)

106   For an examination of U.S. media coverage of the Gulf War, see the introduction in the paperback edition of *Unreliable Sources.*

107   "make us numb to our...," Schaef, *When Society Becomes an Addict,* p. 93.

108   "in short, means protective...", Orwell, *1984,* p. 175.

108   "holding two contradictory beliefs...," Orwell, *1984,* p. 176.

108   "To tell deliberate lies...," Orwell, *1984,* p. 177.

109   "We know that crimes against...," Lawrence Eagleburger quoted in *Los Angeles Times,* December 17, 1992.

109   "be leading the Desert Storms...," Clinton, May 18, 1991.

110   "one of his finest moments...," *Time,* July 5, 1993.

110   "a near-defiant sense of pride...," *New York Times,* June 28, 1993.

111   "is a truly revolutionary force...," Joyce Nelson, *Sign*

Crimes / Road Kill: From Mediascape to Landscape,
p. 103. A Canadian essayist, Nelson has published
several books with Toronto-based Between The
Lines. Her book *Sultans of Sleaze: Public Relations
and the Media* was published in a U.S. edition by
Common Courage Press.

112   Rose Goldsen quoted in Nelson, *Sign Crimes / Road
Kill,* p. 103, from Goldsen's book *The Show & Tell
Machine.*

Chapter Six:
The White House of "the Middle Class"

113   "people earning more than $115,000...," *New York
Times,* July 31, 1993.

114   "The jury is still out on...," Robert Reich quoted in
New York Times, August 8, 1993.

115   "Unions are O.K. where they...," Ron Brown quoted
in *New York Times,* August 8, 1993.

116   "kicked us in the teeth," William F. Gibson quoted
in *New York Times,* July 14, 1993.

116   "transformed the original goals of...," Lani Guinier
writing in a 1991 *Michigan Law Review* article,
quoted by Bruce Shapiro, the *Nation,* May 31,
1993.

116   "Guinier advocates a profoundly democratic...,"
Bruce Shapiro, the *Nation,* May 31, 1993.

116   "This cave-in is a betrayal...," Leslie Harris quoted
in *New York Times* article headlined "Words and
Deeds," June 6, 1993.

116   Clinton may have been emotionally shaken on the
day he dropped the nomination of Lani Guinier, but
he seemed more upset about the personal dynamics than the principles involved. After announcing

his decision, Clinton went to a White House dinner where, according to *Time* (June 14, 1993), he informed guests that "I love her" and added: "If she called me and told me she needed $5,000, I'd take it from my account and send it to her, no questions asked." But Guinier wasn't looking for a handout.

117   "for failing to be a team ...," *Time*, June 14, 1993.

117   "We didn't come all...," Fannie Lou Hamer, quoted in the documentary film "Eyes on the Prize."

117   "It may not satisfy everybody...," Walter Mondale, footage in the documentary film "Eyes on the Prize." Decades later, interviewed for the film, Mondale was still defending the national Democratic Party's response to the challenge by the Mississippi Freedom Democratic Party: "It had to be resolved, it had to be compromised I think in the way that we did it, and it was inevitable that some people would be unhappy."

118   "In liberal circles the MFDP's rejection...," Nicolaus Mills, *Like a Holy Crusade*, p. 160.

118   "It is plainly difficult for...," Anthony Lewis, quoted in *Like a Holy Crusade*, p. 161.

118   "We learned the hard way...," Fannie Lou Hamer quoted in *The Eyes on the Prize Civil Rights Reader*, p. 179. The book published excerpts from her 1967 autobiography.

119   "We were asserting a moral...," Charles Sherrod quoted in *The Eyes on the Prize Civil Rights Reader*, p. 189.

120   Clinton's ditching of Guinier came only days after he appointed David Gergen to be the top media maven at the White House. The contrast in media coverage was illuminating. Political journalists lavished praise on Gergen as nonideological, but the

spin was quite different about Guinier. On June 6, 1993, a *New York Times* "news analysis" by reporter Michael Kelly explained: "In choosing the 43-year-old law professor to be assistant attorney general for civil rights, President Clinton chose not just an old friend but an ideologue, someone with a set of passionately held, explicitly expressed ideas about race and power that were welcomed by the left wing of the Democratic Party but which appalled the party's middle and right."

120 For a cogent look at the news media slant on the Lani Guinier nomination, see article in *Extra!,* July/August 1993, and "Correction" in *Extra!,* September/October 1993.

120 "The Guinier debacle was damaging...," Editorial Notebook, *New York Times,* June 21, 1993.

122 "It's clear to the religious right...," Log Cabin Republicans leader Rich Tafel, quoted in *New York Times,* July 21, 1993.

124 *San Francisco Chronicle,* July 12, 1993.

125 Charles King was interviewed on "Convention Watch," July 13, 1992 (national broadcast from WBAI Radio in New York).

126 "In an effort to be seen...," Committee for Health Rights in Central America (347 Dolores St., #210, San Francisco, CA 94110), Urgent Action Alert, August 4, 1993.

126 When Barbara Boxer responded to economic fears in 1993 by blaming immigrants, she was adding to popular misconceptions about immigration. "You wouldn't know it from most news coverage, but immigrants—whether legal or illegal—benefit the U.S. economy, according to studies gathered by the Reagan and Bush administrations," Jeff Cohen and I pointed out in our syndicated weekly column

(*Seattle Times*, August 7, 1993). "Immigrants spur investment and job creation, work hard at often-unwanted jobs, and pay more in taxes than they take out in government services. An exceptional *Business Week* cover story in July 1992, 'Immigrants: How They're Helping the Economy,' reported that 'immigrants pay an estimated $90 billion in taxes, compared with the $5 billion in welfare benefits they receive.' States with heavy immigration do carry increased school, health and welfare costs, but it's not because immigrants are ripping off the system. The problem is that the federal government doesn't share its windfall of immigrant taxes with the states most impacted."

127   "as the months went on...," *New York Times*, June 27, 1993. Added the *Times*: "Colleen Conway-Welch, dean of the Vanderbilt School of Nursing and a member of the President's Commission on AIDS in the Reagan administration, of which Ms. [Kristine] Gebbie was also a member, said the new AIDS czar was 'the ultimate consensus builder.'.... Dr. David Rogers, co-chairman of the current National Commission on AIDS, said he was also pleased with her nomination, but he, too, was cautious. 'There is the potential for a lot of nasty politics here, and it has plagued us throughout the epidemic,' he said. '....She is a consensus-builder and can succeed, but it is absolutely dependent on whether the president gives this job the authority it needs....'"

127   As months went by without selection of an "AIDS czar," the White House disregarded the pleas of its associate director of personnel, Bob Hattoy. He recalled: "I got a note back from a White House official, after I was jumping up and down about the fact there was no AIDS czar, to 'quit pestering' her about the AIDS czar." Hattoy, a gay man with AIDS,

told a reporter he considered the note to be "condescending and insulting." (*New York Times Magazine,* June 6, 1993.) The previous summer, Hattoy—an environmental adviser to the Clinton campaign—addressed the Democratic National Convention only weeks after being diagnosed with AIDS. The speech was eloquent and moving. Yet I found its class tilt more than a little troubling. People with AIDS, he said, "are doctors and lawyers, folks in the military, ministers, rabbis and priests. We are Democrats, and yes, Mr. President, Republicans. We're part of the American family. Yes, Mr. President, your family has AIDS. We're dying, and you're doing nothing about it." True enough; but Hattoy's speech seemed so intent on making people with AIDS seem respectable that it left unmentioned the realities that some people— black, Latino, poor—are suffering from AIDS in proportions much higher than their numbers in the U.S. population.

128 Helen Rodriguez-Trias was interviewed on "Convention Watch," July 13, 1992.

129 A passing reference to Ruth Bader Ginsburg in the *New York Times* (June 27, 1993) provided clues as to her judicial inclinations: "During her thirteen years on the appeals court, Judge Ginsburg often sided with the more conservative judges appointed by Presidents Ronald Reagan and George Bush. According to a computerized study of the appeals court's 1987 voting patterns published in *Legal Times,* Judge Ginsburg voted more consistently with her Republican-appointed colleagues than with her fellow Democratic-appointed colleagues." In August 1993, only three senators voted against her when Ginsburg won confirmation to the U.S. Supreme Court.

129 Zoë Baird's background included lobbying against health-care reform. Other aspects of her corporate record were also notably retrograde. As *Time* reported (February 1, 1993), "public-interest advocates quietly voiced their reservations" about the nomination of Baird for attorney general. "Broadly, they worried about Baird's stance on tort reform; specifically, they questioned her role in Aetna's campaign to restrict the number of civil suits brought against corporations. Critics also pointed to Baird's work at GE that led to implementation of a program aimed at dodging federal prosecution and blunting whistle blowing on waste and contract fraud. With the notable exception of consumer watchdog Ralph Nader, most of the carping was done anonymously. A public-interest activist explained the general reluctance to openly criticize Clinton's nominee: 'The Washington civil rights lobby groups have a symbiotic relationship with the Democratic Party and are unwilling to rock the boat. They are desperate to preserve their access.'"

129 "For all the talk of 'change,'" commented the *Washington Spectator* (April 1, 1993), "this cabinet is decidedly establishmentarian. Ten of the fourteen cabinet members are lawyers, as many as ten are millionaires and several are implicated in the savings and loan and corporate takeover scandals of the Reagan-Bush era."

129 "Although whites who bring blacks...," Roger Wilkins, *A Man's Life,* p. 330.

130 "Yet Turkey's human rights picture...," Lois Whitman, letter, *New York Times,* June 27, 1993.

131 "collateral damage," quoted on NPR News ("All Things Considered"), June 27, 1993.

131 For a debunking of the alleged Iraqi conspiracy to

kill Bush during his visit to Kuwait, see Patrick Cockburn's article "The Plot Thins," *In These Times,* August 9, 1993 (excerpted from the *Independent* newspaper in Britain). A companion article by Miles Harvey added that "in an informal survey of the country's leading news outlets, *In These Times* could find no attempts to independently confirm the administration's charges of Iraqi involvement in the bombing plot."

132   Clinton request that Congress boost the CIA budget was reported in *New York Times,* April 15, 1993.

132   "turned many southern Lebanese villages...," *New York Times,* August 1, 1993.

133   "There's nobody better...," James Baker quoted in *New York Times,* July 16, 1993. The *Times* interviewed others from the Bush team who commented on how Dennis Ross epitomized the continuity of Middle East policies between Republican and Democratic administrations. Former Bush aide James Pinkerton said that Clinton's decision to retain Ross on the White House payroll was "like conquering somebody's country and then turning to one of their generals and saying: 'Hey, why don't you stick around? And by the way, what do you think we should do now?'" A staffer for Ross during the Bush administration, Andrew Carpendale, remarked that "in many ways his policy interests in the peace process transcend political affiliation."

134   "a firestorm of public opinion," quoted in War Resisters League magazine *The Nonviolent Activist,* September/October 1993.

134   Hiroshima Day 1993 statement available from Peninsula Peace and Justice Center, P.O. Box 1725, Palo Alto, CA 94302.

135   Liane Clorfene-Casten, "E.P.A. Fiddles While W.T.I.

Burns," the *Nation*, September 27, 1993.

137   Gar Smith interview, September 10, 1993.

138   "threatens to achieve victories over...," Alexander Cockburn, the *Nation*, September 6/13, 1993.

139   "NAFTA is, in fact, little more...," Melvin Burke, the *Humanist*, September/October 1993. Burke, a professor of economics at the University of Maine, also wrote in his article: "It is abundantly clear that NAFTA will give rise to a major redistribution of income and wealth—not so much from country to country as from one socioeconomic class to another. More specifically, NAFTA will undoubtedly redistribute income from wage and salaried workers to the propertied elite in Mexico, Canada, and the United States."

Chapter Seven:
Liberal Haze and the Centrist Dream

142   Martin Luther King Jr. broke his public silence on the Vietnam War when he spoke in Los Angeles on February 25, 1967. Media denunciations of his anti-war stand grew fierce after his speech at Riverside Church in New York City on April 4, 1967. In response to the disputes of the day about how much social spending could be maintained in light of the war in Vietnam, King was adamant that "when a nation becomes obsessed with the guns of war, social programs must inevitably suffer. We can talk about guns and butter all we want to, but when the guns are there with all of its emphasis you don't even get good oleo. These are facts of life."

144   "Among various income groups...," Dr. Gregory Pappas quoted in *New York Times*, July 8, 1993.

144   "socioeconomic status is a powerful...," *New*

England Journal of Medicine, July 8, 1993. The editorial accompanied the journal's publication of data from the National Center for Health Statistics report.

144   "The death rate for...," *New York Times,* July 8, 1993.

144   At the end of the 1980s, Jonathan Kozol wrote, "the gap between white and black mortality in children" was at a new record. "Black children are more than twice as likely to die in infancy as whites—nine times as likely to be neurologically impaired." As Kozol put it, the economic status quo "condemns the children of the very poor to the implacable inheritance of a diminished destiny." (Kozol's article appeared in a special issue of *Newsweek,* Winter/Spring 1990.)

145   Joint Economic Committee estimate of poverty, *Washington Post,* October 30, 1989.

146   "the fraudulent and expedient nature...," James Baldwin, *No Name in the Street,* p. 188.

147   "out-of-wedlock births to teenagers...," Joe Klein, *Newsweek,* April 26, 1993.

148   The article quoting Al From appeared in the *New York Times* of July 8, 1993 under the headline "Perot's Support Is Here to Stay, Pollster Reports." Interestingly the twenty-four paragraph article made no mention of race, although nuanced white racial antipathies spearheaded by the DLC were hardly opaque. The article quoted From as recommending that Clinton "take a welfare reform package and push it through [Congress], even if there's opposition within his own party." Al From had served as a deputy adviser to President Carter during the latter part of his term. Says key Clinton adviser Paul Begala: "Every oyster needs a grain of

sand to make a pearl. Al From is the grain of sand that made the Clinton candidacy." (Begala was quoted in *Time*, December 14, 1992.)

148 "'Reagan Democrats'...," Manning Marable, the *Progressive*, November 1992.

148 "The campaign has sent out...," Adolph Reed Jr., the *Progressive*, November 1992.

149 "based on an appeal...," Herbert Hill, the *Progressive*, November 1992.

149 "rhetoric of 'personal responsibility'...," Adolph Reed Jr., the *Progressive*, November 1992.

150 "It's time to shift...," Charles Robb, April 12, 1986.

150 "If we are going to be...," Clinton, statement issued June 1991.

150 "We're going to empower people...," Clinton quoted in *Time*, November 16, 1992.

150 "if we give opportunity without...," Bill Clinton, May 6, 1991. The speech reminded colleagues in the Democratic Leadership Council: "Our DLC has over 600 federal, state and local elected officials, people who are brimming with ideas, people who are out there on the firing line every day, actually solving problems and somehow getting the electoral support they need to go forward."

153 "And so I will choose...," June Jordan, the *Progressive*, November 1992.

153 After more than three months in office, President Clinton announced a plan that the *New York Times* (May 5, 1993) described as his "first to address the poorest Americans." It was a pitiful plan: A measly $1.6 billion—less than the cost of the B-2 Bomber in the 1994 budget—would be devoted to poor neighborhoods during each of the next five years.

Half of the $1.6 billion would go to business tax credits, with most of the rest refocusing old programs rather than providing more funds. Such emphasis on "enterprise zones" and "empowerment zones" perpetuated the myth that scattered private investment could halt poverty. The White House talked about adding social-services coordination to the mix, but it advocated only paltry funding for those services. Starved of funds, the government programs can only be band-aids for deadly conditions.

153   "Mayors, who were clamoring...," *New York Times,* July 9, 1993. The news article was headlined "The Cities Are Scraping By, but at a Cost."

153   "the futility of complaint...," *Newsweek,* July 5, 1993.

154   Donald Fraser quoted in *New York Times,* July 9, 1993.

154   Emory Curtis, *California Voice,* August 27, 1993. He noted: "Funding for the empowerment zones consists of $2.5 billion for employer wage credits and $720 million for two years of spending on child care, worker training, education, etc. Total social spending for the enterprise zone program is $280 million; no funding is available for enterprise zone employer wage credits."

155   Daniel Patrick Moynihan's memo to Nixon, intended as a confidential communication, was leaked in early 1970, about a year after it was written. Five presidents and uncounted urban disasters later, Moynihan was well-positioned to further his belief in "benign neglect" as the Democrat chairing the Senate Finance Committee.

155   "was an attack on...," William Greider, *Who Will Tell the People,* p. 263.

156 "divided by nasty ideological...," William Greider, *Who Will Tell the People*, p. 263. Greider added: "The party elite had no intention of sharing its own policy deliberations with Democrats at large or trying to re-engage people in governing politics by rebuilding the organizational connections that have been lost. The elites wished only to form a governing consensus around the supposed 'mainstream'— their mainstream, the one they have already formulated in Washington."

157 "middle course...," *Newsweek*, March 30, 1992

157 "the party's most...," Joe Klein, *Newsweek*, September 7, 1992

157 "After a decade of Reaganism...," Manning Marable, the *Progressive*, November 1992. During Clinton's first year as president, his symbols sometimes underscored the truth of Marable's observation that the conservative agenda of the Democratic Leadership Council "represents a sharp break from the New Deal-Great Society liberalism." In a story about Clinton's boating party off Martha's Vineyard, the *New York Times* (August 25, 1993) reported: "By the time Mr. Clinton returned to shore in the late afternoon, he had changed out of the preppy open-neck polo shirt he wore in the morning into a T-shirt inscribed with the initials of the Democratic Leadership Council, the organization of centrist Southerners who helped elect him by wresting the Democratic Party away from the liberal theories Senator [Edward] Kennedy had espoused."

157 "They're a new generation...," Clinton-Gore TV ad quoted in the *Progressive*, December 1992.

158 "The times they are a-changin' back" was a campaign slogan for the fictionalized politician Bob

Roberts, portrayed by Tim Robbins in the superb 1992 movie "Bob Roberts."

Chapter Eight:
Enabling the Status Quo

164   While "The Simpsons" has been among the clever-
est and most enjoyable programs on network TV in
recent years, some appreciative viewers go over-
board—projecting personal responses, and exagger-
ating the profundity of what the show conveys to
the mass audience. In the *Nation* (April 5, 1993),
film critic Stuart Klawans wrote that he'd "like to
see a critical theory and practice of mass media
that will acknowledge the liberating power of 'The
Simpsons.'" But the sum of the show is far less
than the best rapid-fire parts might seem to por-
tend; the moments of "liberating power" are largely
counteracted by the ambiguities that abound within and around the weekly program. Satiric depictions of a dysfunctional society don't necessarily do
much to undermine its negative dynamics—especially when the satire is so intertwined with messages that could be heard as reinforcing the types
of violence and commercialization being lam-
pooned.

166   "Our third book was our first...," Earthworks Press
eight-page brochure (undated), titled: "A 50 Simple
Things Book: A Premium Book with a Positive
Message." (Mailing address: Earthworks Press,
1400 Shattuck Ave., #25, Berkeley, CA 94709.)

166   "the American social conscience seems...," Jack
Kroll, *Newsweek,* April 2, 1990.

167   *In These Times,* letters, August 9, 1993.

168   Michiko Kakutani, "Against the Tide: Making a

Case for Shades of Gray," *New York Times,* June 18, 1993.

168   In exploring "propaganda from the center," I am indebted to the insights of my friend and colleague Jeff Cohen, executive director of the media watch group FAIR. For his perceptive essay on the subject, see *Extra!,* October/November 1989.

169   For another article by Michiko Kakutani that labored to conflate very different political outlooks—on the grounds that they all embodied "revisionist" and "deconstructionist" trends—see the *New York Times* of April 30, 1993. Under the headline "When History Is a Casualty," Kakutani expended 2,469 words to draw parallels between denying the Holocaust and other "revisionism"— such as debunking the Warren Commission, and depicting "the settling of the American West" as "the violent westward march of greedy, genocidal land-robbers." Displayed at the top of the front page of the *Times* "Living Arts" section, the essay lamented that "politically correct histories" now portray Columbus's arrival in America "as the beginning of an imperial rape of an Edenic world." Properly stressing that the genocide set in motion by Hitler must not be understated, the article proceeded to mock those who stress that the genocide set in motion by Columbus must not be understated. With conventional depictions of the past under assault from a multitude of directions, Kakutani seemed to imply that deniers of untrue "history" can be faulted for egging on deniers of true history. (She concluded: "Together with society's current eagerness to blur the lines between fact and fantasy, reality and appearance, the deconstructionists and like-minded thinkers foster a climate in which ideologues and propagandists, like the Holocaust deniers, can try to assail those two pillars of

human civilization: memory and truth." It might have been valuable for Kakutani to apply her zeal for "memory and truth" to the continuing failure of U.S. society to come to terms with what the U.S. government did to people in Vietnam, Laos and Cambodia. But no such luck.) Thematic equation of "extremes" reappeared, more explicitly, in her later article "Against the Tide: Making a Case for Shades of Gray," *New York Times,* June 18, 1993.

171   "We've got to have...," Bill Clinton, May 6, 1991.

171   "shabby, gutless performance...," Christopher Hitchens, the *Nation,* July 5, 1993.

171   "pattern reflects two contradictory impulses...," *New York Times,* August 15, 1993.

173   As 1993 began, *Time* (January 4) declared: "The Clinton reinvention—if it succeeds—will bring his baby-boom generation (so insufferable in so many ways, and so unavoidable) to full harvest, to the power and responsibility that they clamored to overthrow in the streets a quarter of a century ago."

173   As an alert "New Democrat," Clinton didn't lose much time "reinventing" himself as a tolerant Ross Perot. While presenting extended erudite essays in contrast to Ross's dumbed-down squibs, and proving himself with semi-automatic deficit sharpshooting alongside Perot's full-bore reports, Clinton could be as culturally loose as Perot was uptight, as intellectually perky as Perot was shallow; and yet Clinton seemed determined to stay within shouting distance of the billionaire "populist," whistling his tune past whatever political graveyard threatened to be getting too close for comfort.

173   News media struck some bemused poses in response to White House rhetoric about "reinvention," but went on to purvey such babble them-

selves. So, in a photo caption on September 9, 1993, the *New York Times* matter-of-factly reported: "Mr. Gore and President Clinton plan once again to take their road show around the country this week to push for reinventing government."

174   For a discussion of "political correctness" and mass media, see *Adventures in Medialand,* pp. 88-91.

174   One of the main charges leveled against unauthorized complainers has been undue preoccupation with power. "What used to be understood as modes of courtship are now seen as modes of male intimidation," Allan Bloom wrote in *Love and Friendship* as he inveighed against "the imperial project of reform promoted by radical feminism." Bloom deplored trends toward clarity about existing power relationships: "The worst distortion of all is to turn love, a relation that is founded in natural sweetness, mutual caring and the contemplation of eternity in shared children, into a power struggle.... Everything that used to be thought natural must now be overcome in the name of abstract equality." Providing some unintended irony when it excerpted Bloom's book, the *New York Times Magazine* (May 23, 1993) printed climactic paragraphs above a half-page ad showing a woman with a cigarette in her hand, next to the slogan "Portraits of Pleasure."

174   "Silence is not golden...," Nikky Finney, commencement address at Mills College, Oakland, California, May 23, 1993. The text of her speech appeared in *Mills Quarterly,* July 1993.

176   "Americans have generally regarded...," *New York Times,* August 15, 1993. The article identified an unfortunate shortage of paternalism in Bill Clinton's demeanor during the first seven months of his presidency: "In appearance and manner, Mr. Clinton has played more the role of a brother or

even a son."

179   Of course partisan fervor encourages the faithful to
       deny history as convenient. At the 1988 Democratic
       National Convention in Atlanta, I had a long con-
       versation with a young Democratic Party staffer
       who insisted—with apparent earnestness—that the
       Republican Party was responsible for getting the
       United States into the Vietnam War. To hear him
       tell it, Democrats had nothing to do with it. If dead
       men could put PR flacks on retainer, JFK and LBJ
       would have done well to hire him on the spot.

179   "We took space back quickly...," Michael Herr,
       Dispatches, p. 71.

180   "never found a way to...," Michael Herr, *Dispatches*,
       p. 215.

Chapter Nine:
"The Fierce Urgency of *Now*"

181   "We are now faced...," Martin Luther King Jr.,
       Where Do We Go from Here: Chaos or Community?,
       p. 191. In this book—his last—King wrote: "The
       curse of poverty has no justification in our age. It is
       socially as cruel and blind as the practice of canni-
       balism at the dawn of civilization, when men ate
       each other because they had not yet learned to take
       food from the soil or to consume the abundant ani-
       mal life around them. The time has come for us to
       civilize ourselves by the total, direct and immediate
       abolition of poverty." (Pp. 165-66.) He added: "The
       time has come for an all-out world war against
       poverty. The rich nations must use their vast
       resources of wealth to develop the underdeveloped,
       school the unschooled and feed the unfed. The
       well-off and the secure have too often become indif-
       ferent and oblivious to the poverty and deprivation

in their midst. The poor in our countries have been shut out of our minds, and driven from the mainstream of our societies, because we have allowed them to become invisible. Ultimately a great nation is a compassionate nation. No individual or nation can be great if it does not have a concern for 'the least of these.'" (P. 178.)

182   "Our only hope today lies...," *Where Do We Go from Here: Chaos or Community?,* p. 190 and p. 191.

186   "If there is no struggle...," Frederick Douglass quoted in Howard Zinn, *A People's History of the United States,* p. 179.

186   "You're in charge, but...," Bobbie Walker quoted in *New York Times,* August 21, 1993. The article added: "What is happening in towns like this is happening in small towns across America."

188   Writing in the *Nation* (September 6/13, 1993), health policy specialist Vicente Navarro noted that the man "considered the main intellectual force behind managed competition" is Alain Enthoven— "deputy to Defense Secretary Robert McNamara during the Vietnam War, supervisor of the 'body count' method of evaluating military efficiency in that conflict and now a professor of business administration at Stanford." Enthoven was a leader of the Jackson Hole Group that came up with "managed competition" scenarios; others in the Jackson Hole Group included emissaries from big insurance companies such as Prudential, Metropolitan Life, Aetna and Cigna. The options put forward by the group, Navarro wrote, "represent the response of not only the insurance industry but other segments of corporate America to the crisis in costs and legitimacy of the health care sector. They are part of what the *New York Times* calls the new consensus for reform. Michael Weinstein, a

disciple of Enthoven and a member of the editorial board of the *Times*, has written nine editorials extolling the virtues of managed competition." Out of the dozen members of the *Times* board of directors, four are also directors of major insurance companies; two are directors of pharmaceutical companies. (When Jeff Cohen and I wrote a syndicated column on media coverage of health-care options, it appeared in the *Seattle Times* on May 15, 1993, under the apt headline: "Managed competition; managed news.")

189　"It's very hard to get...," Noam Chomsky, *The Chomsky Reader*, p. 49.

192　"In this unfolding conundrum...," *Where Do We Go from Here: Chaos or Community?*, p. 191.

192　Franz Kafka, *The Trial* (Schocken Books edition), pp. 213-15.

Acknowledgments

Many people offered ideas and information for this book.

My friend Jeff Cohen went over drafts in detail; as always, his advice was very valuable. Two other people at the media watch group FAIR—Janine Jackson and Jim Naureckas—also provided astute critiques of the manuscript.

Strong encouragement came from Victor Wallis, who pointed out many ways that I could improve the work-in-progress. Jennifer Warburg went extra miles to be supportive of this book. And Greg Saatkamp gave his perspectives. So did my buddy Walt Curtis.

Shea Dean did key research with creative skill and perseverance.

Each in a unique way, my parents Miriam and Morris, my sister Helen, and my brothers Abba and Eugene have been encouraging.

From the outset, Greg Bates expressed a clear commitment to bringing out *False Hope.* He showed himself to be adept at dialogue, and the book is much better as a result. In the process of building Common Courage Press, he and Flic Shooter have been nurturing precious resources for us all.

I'd also like to thank my literary agent, Laura Gross, for her assistance.

Throughout the writing of *False Hope*, I had the great fortune to be near Cheryl Higgins, a fine editor and an all-around superb companion. Her love sustains me beyond measure.

About the Author

Norman Solomon's previous books include *Adventures in Medialand: Behind the News, Beyond the Pundits* (Common Courage Press, 1993), co-authored with Jeff Cohen; *The Power of Babble: The Politician's Dictionary of Buzzwords and Doubletalk for Every Occasion* (Dell Publishing, 1992); *Unreliable Sources: A Guide to Detecting Bias in News Media* (Carol Publishing, 1990), co-authored with Martin A. Lee; and *Killing Our Own: The Disaster of America's Experience With Atomic Radiation* (Delacorte/Delta, 1982), co-authored with Harvey Wasserman.

Solomon's political articles have appeared in publications ranging from the *Progressive*, the *Nation* and *Utne Reader* to the *New York Times, USA Today, Los Angeles Times* and *International Herald Tribune*. With Jeff Cohen, he writes a nationally-syndicated column on media and politics, distributed by Creators Syndicate and AlterNet.

An associate of FAIR, the media watch organization, Solomon lives in the San Francisco area, and speaks to audiences around the country. He can be contacted via the publisher: Common Courage Press, Box 702, Monroe, ME 04951; (207) 525-0900.

Doug Henwood is a contributing editor of the *Nation* magazine. He is the editor of *Left Business Observer,* a monthly newsletter on economics and politics worldwide. (Subscriptions are available for $20 a year from: *Left Business Observer,* 250 West 85th St., New York, NY 10024.)

Index

Index

Index

Index

172, 202, 206, 228, 229, 231
Democratic National Committee, 50, 172, 199
Democratic National Convention (1964), 65, 117-20
Democratic National Convention (1968), 77, 213
Democratic National Convention (1972), 77
Democratic National Convention (1984), 86
Democratic National Convention (1988), 41, 51-53, 88, 210, 236
Democratic National Convention (1992), 33, 39, 50, 53, 151, 152, 209, 224
Democratic Party, 9, 28, 32, 33, 53, 84, 86, 87-88, 125, 148, 150-51, 152, 155-56, 157, 158, 171, 183, 188, 191, 206, 225, 236
Democratic Party Platform (1992), 32, 125, 151, 152
Democrats, 20, 21, 28, 34, 42, 44, 48, 54, 56, 65, 67, 68, 86-87, 109, 113, 115, 121, 123, 126, 146, 148, 150-51, 156, 182, 236
Denmark, 19
"Desert Storms," 109
Detroit, 187
Dickens, Charles, 204-5

Dionne, E.J., Jr., 53-58
Disney TV shows, 63
Dole, Bob, 160, 168
Donaldson, Sam, 160
Douglass, Frederick, 186
Dow Chemical, 27
Dukakis, Michael, 9, 41, 52, 88, 149, 200, 210
Dulles, John Foster, 22
Dunlop, John, 115
Du Pont, 137
Duvalier, Jean-Claude, 10, 51
Dylan, Bob, 214

E

Eagleburger, Lawrence, 109
Earned Income Tax Credit, 12
Earth Day, 165
Earth Island Journal, 137
Earthworks Press, 166
East Liverpool (Ohio), 135
East Timor, 81-82, 95
Economic Policy Institute, 14
Economist, The, 9
Eden, 138, 169, 233
Ehrenreich, Barbara, 197, 206-7
Eisenhower, Dwight, 22
Eizenstat, Stuart, 28
El Salvador, 82, 83, 85, 121, 214-15
Electoral College, 55
Ellsberg, Daniel, 67, 76
Encyclopedia Britannica, 178

Index

Energy Department, 134
Enthoven, Alain, 237-38
Environmental Protection
   Agency, 11, 135, 137
Espy, Mike, 129
Europe, 13, 70, 176
Extra!, 201, 222, 233

F

FAIR, 103, 201, 218
"Father Knows Best," 63-
   64, 202
Fauntleroy, Little Lord, 44
Feinstein, Dianne, 126-27
*50 Simple Things You Can
   Do to Save the Earth*, 165
*50 Simple Things Kids Can
   Do to Save the Earth*, 166
Finland, 19
Finney, Nikky, 174
Fire Next Time, The
   (Baldwin), 212
First Amendment, 60
First World, 13, 16
Fleetwood Mac, 172
Flower Power, 69
Foggy Bottom, 47
Forbes, 9
Forbes, Malcolm, 129
Ford, Gerald, 79, 81
Ford administration, 115
France, 17, 19
Fraser, Donald, 154
Freeze campaign, 85-89
Fried, Bruce, 124
Friedman, Milton, 9
Friedman, Thomas L., 25
From, Al, 148, 228-29

Fromm, Erich, 216

G

Gates, Daryl, 217
Gebbie, Kristine, 127, 223
Gelb, Leslie, 48
General Electric, 129, 225
Georgia Pacific, 27
Gergen, David, 28, 29-30,
   196, 198, 221
Germany, 13, 17, 19, 70
Gibson, William F., 116
Ginsburg, Ruth Bader, 129,
   224
God, 65, 145
Goldman Sachs, 10, 20
Goldscheid, Rudolf, 12
Goldsen, Rose, 112
Goldwater, Barry, 66
Goodman, Michael J., 15
G.O.P. *See* Republican
   Party
Gore, Al, 44, 135-37, 153,
   157, 235
Gorelick, Jamie S., 208
Gramm, Phil, 205
Gray, Billy, 63-64
Great Expectations
   (Dickens), 204-5
Great Society, 66, 157, 231
Greer, Frank, 44
Greider, William, 155-56,
   231
Groening, Matt, 164-65
Gross Domestic Product
   (GDP), 11, 13
Guatemala, 82, 85
Guevara, Ernesto "Che," 69

Index

Index

Index

Index

"Morning Edition," 103
Moscow, 133
Moseley-Braun, Carol, 188
Mother Jones, 36, 207
Moynihan, Daniel Patrick, 155, 230
Muir, John, 138
MX, 80, 214, 216

N

N.A.A.C.P., 116
Nabisco, 166
Nader, Ralph, 225
NASA, 41, 65
Nation, 116, 136-37, 171, 197, 232, 237-38
National Center for Health Statistics, 144
National Guard, 66
National Labor Relations Board, 114
National League of Cities, 154
National Security Council, 132
Native Americans, 34, 71, 146, 190
Navarro, Vicente, 237-38
Nazis, 77, 169
Nelson, Joyce, 111, 220
Nervous Nellies, 68
Nevada Test Site, 190
New Deal, 149, 157, 231
New Democrats, 34, 54, 152, 153, 171, 234
New England Journal of Medicine, 144, 201
New Left, 68, 72

New World, 169
New York Times, 25, 29, 48, 93, 110, 113, 118, 120, 127, 132, 144, 147, 153, 168, 171, 176, 196, 203, 222, 223, 224, 229, 231, 233-34, 235, 237, 237-38
New York Times Magazine, 201-2, 224, 235
Newspeak, 92, 110
Newsweek, 29, 30, 44, 147, 153, 157, 166, 208, 209, 228
Nicaragua, 82, 85, 215
Nieman Reports, 216-17
1984 (Orwell), 91, 92, 94, 108-9, 216
Nixon, Richard, 40, 46, 76, 79, 81, 83, 104-5, 148, 155, 230
Nixon administration, 46
Nixon Agonistes (Wills), 22
No Name in the Street (Baldwin), 212
North American Free Trade Agreement (NAFTA), 14, 139, 201, 227
Northern Hemisphere, 16
Norway, 17, 19
NPR, 103, 218

O

Ohio, 76, 135
O'Leary, Hazel, 129
Onassis, Jacqueline Kennedy, 204
O'Neill, Tip, 34
Organization for Economic

Index

Index

Index

Index